SPECTRUM

4

GEORGIA
Test Prep

Align
to Achieve
The Academic Standards e-Library

SPECTRUM

Frank Schaffer Publications®

Spectrum is an imprint of Frank Schaffer Publications.

Printed in the United States of America. All rights reserved. Except as permitted under the United States Copyright Act, no part of this publication may be reproduced or distributed in any form or by any means, or stored in a database or retrieval system, without prior written permission from the publisher, unless otherwise indicated. Frank Schaffer Publications is an imprint of School Specialty Publishing. Copyright © 2006 School Specialty Publishing.

Send all inquiries to:
Frank Schaffer Publications
8720 Orion Place
Columbus, Ohio 43240-2111

ISBN 0-7696-3474-5

3 4 5 6 7 8 9 10 COR 11 10 09 08 07 06

Table of Contents

What's Inside?

This workbook is designed to help you and your fourth grader understand what he or she will be expected to know on the Georgia fourth-grade state tests.

Practice Pages

The workbook is divided into four sections: English/Language Arts, Mathematics, Social Studies, and Science. Each section has practice activities that have questions similar to those that will appear on the state tests. Students should use a pencil to fill in the correct answers and to complete any writing on these activities.

Georgia State Standards

Before each practice section is a list of the state standards covered by that section. The shaded *What it means* sections will help to explain any information in the standards that might be unfamiliar.

Mini-Tests and Final Tests

Practice activities are grouped by state standard. When each group is completed, the student can move on to a mini-test that covers the material presented on those practice activities. After an entire set of standards and accompanying activities are completed, the student should take the final tests, which incorporates materials from all the practice activities in that section.

Final Test Answer Sheet

The final tests have a separate answer sheet that mimics the style of the answer sheets the students will use on the state tests. The answer sheets appear at the end of each final test.

How Am I Doing?

These pages are designed to help students identify areas where they are proficient and areas where they still need more practice. Students can keep track of each of their mini-test scores on these pages.

Answer Key

Answers to all the practice activities, mini-tests, and final tests are listed by page number and appear at the end of the book.

Frequently Asked Questions

What kinds of information does my child have to know to pass the test?

The Georgia Department of Education provides a list of the knowledge and skills that students are expected to master at each grade level. The activities in this workbook provide students with practice in each of these areas.

Are there special strategies or tips that will help my child do well?

The workbook provides sample questions that have content similar to that on the state tests. Test-taking tips are offered throughout the book.

How do I know what areas my child needs help in?

A special *How Am I Doing?* section will help you and your fourth grader evaluate progress. It will pinpoint areas where more work is needed as well as areas where your student excels.

Georgia English/Language Arts
Content Standards

The English/Language Arts section measures knowledge in four different areas:

1) Reading

2) Writing

3) Conventions

4) Listening, Speaking, and Viewing

Georgia English/Language Arts
Table of Contents

Reading Standards

In reading a text closely, the student works carefully to discern the author's perspective and the particular facts and details that support it. The student reads thoughtfully and purposefully, constantly checking for understanding of the author's intent and meaning so that the interpretation will be sound.

ELA4R1. The student demonstrates comprehension and shows evidence of a warranted and responsible explanation of a variety of literary and informational texts. The texts are of the quality and complexity illustrated by the Grade Four Reading List, located on page 24. *(See pages 8–20.)*

For literary texts, the student identifies the characteristics of various genres and produces evidence of reading that:
a. relates theme in works of fiction and nonfiction to personal experience.
b. identifies and analyzes the elements of plot, character, and setting in stories read, written, viewed, or performed.
c. identifies the speaker of a poem or story.
d. identifies sensory details and figurative language.
e. identifies and shows the relevance of foreshadowing clues.

What it means:
- **Figurative language** is language used for descriptive effect. It describes or implies meaning, rather than directly stating it.
- **Foreshadowing** means to indicate that something, usually something unpleasant, is going to happen.

f. makes judgments and inferences about setting, characters, and events and supports them with elaborating and convincing evidence from the text.
g. identifies similarities and differences between the characters or events and theme in a literary work and the actual experiences in an author's life.
h. identifies themes and lessons in folktales, tall tales, and fables.
i. identifies rhyme and rhythm, repetition, similes, and sensory images in poems.

What it means:
- Students should know that **similes** are a type of figurative language that use *like* or *as* to compare things that may seem unlike each other. Example: Her smile was as dazzling as the sun.

For informational texts, the student reads and comprehends in order to develop understanding and expertise and produces evidence of reading that:
a. locates facts that answer the reader's questions.
b. identifies and uses knowledge of common textual features (e.g., paragraphs, topic sentences, concluding sentences, glossary).
c. identifies and uses knowledge of common graphic features (e.g., charts, maps, diagrams, illustrations).
d. identifies and uses knowledge of common organizational structures (e.g., chronological order, cause and effect).
e. distinguishes cause from effect in context.
f. summarizes main ideas and supporting details.
g. makes perceptive and well-developed connections.
h. distinguishes fact from opinion or fiction.

Reading Standards

ELA4R2. The student consistently reads at least twenty-five books or book equivalents (approximately 1,000,000 words) each year. The quality and complexity of the materials to be read are illustrated in the sample reading list, located on page 24. The materials should include traditional and contemporary literature (both fiction and nonfiction) as well as magazines, newspapers, textbooks, and electronic material. Such reading should represent a diverse collection of material from at least three different literary forms and from at least five different writers.

Reading Standards ELA4R3 and ELA4R4 *(See pages 23–24.)*

**English/
Language Arts**

ELA4R1

Identifying Plot

DIRECTIONS: Read the passage and answer the questions that follow.

The Fence

From *The Adventures of Tom Sawyer* by Mark Twain

Saturday morning was come, and all the summer world was bright and fresh, and brimming with life. There was a song in every heart . . . there was cheer in every face and a spring in every step.

Tom appeared on the sidewalk with a bucket of whitewash and a long-handled brush. He surveyed the fence, and all gladness left him and a deep sadness settled down on his spirit. Thirty yards of board fence nine feet high. Life to him seemed hollow, and existence but a burden. Sighing, he dipped his brush and passed it along the topmost plank; repeated the operation; did it again; compared the small streak with the far-reaching continent of fence, and sat down on a tree-box discouraged.

1. **What is the main *conflict,* or problem, in the story?**

   (A) Tom did not know how to sing.

   (B) Tom needed another bucket.

   (C) Tom's brush was not long enough.

   (D) Tom did not want to paint the fence.

2. **What might he decide to do next?**

   (F) spend all day painting the fence

   (G) try to get someone else to paint the fence

   (H) ask for more instructions on painting the fence

   (J) spread paper to keep the paint from dripping

3. **In the story, the mood changes from _____ to _____ as the plot unfolds.**

   (A) cheerful to sad

   (B) cheerful to glad

   (C) sad to hollow

   (D) sad to cheerful

STOP

English/
Language Arts

ELA4R1

Identifying Character Attributes and Motives

DIRECTIONS: Read the story and then answer the questions.

Ralph

Ralph was a dirty mutt. His once-white hair was gray and brown with grime. He wore a dirty collar around his neck that had an old identification tag.

Right now, Ralph was on his belly. His bright, black eyes were glued to a plate at the edge of the table. On it was a ham sandwich. His moist, black nose twitched with the smell. Ralph knew he would get a swat with the broom or spray with the hose if the lady of the house caught him in the yard again.

His empty belly made him brave. The screen door slammed as the lady went back for other goodies. Ralph flew like a bullet to the edge of the table. The plate tipped onto the ground. Ralph grabbed the sandwich with his teeth and he was off. As he dove through a hole in the bushes, water from the hose whitened the back half of his body and his dirty tail.

1. **What is Ralph?**

   mutt

2. **Is Ralph living in a home with people the day he steals the sandwich?**

   yes

3. **Did Ralph have a home at one time? Explain your answer.**

   does not say

4. **What was Ralph's motive for stealing the sandwich?**

   Ralph was on his belly

5. **How does the lady in the passage feel about Ralph? Why do you think this?**

   Crazy because ralph tries to get the sandwich

Identifying Setting

DIRECTIONS: Read the passage and then answer the questions.

At the Water's Edge

Gabe walked down to the water. The sun was setting. The sky was blazing with orange, yellow, pink, and red. At the edge of the water was an odd-looking creature about one-foot long. Its body seemed to be in three parts. A long, hard, pointed tail poked its way out of its body. "What is that thing?" wondered Gabe. "Can it hurt me?"

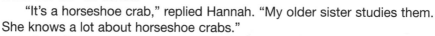

He saw Hannah walking toward him on the beach and called her over. "Do you know what this is?" he asked.

"It's a horseshoe crab," replied Hannah. "My older sister studies them. She knows a lot about horseshoe crabs."

"Great," said Gabe. "I want to know more about them."

1. **What time of day does the story take place?**

   _____

   _____

   _____

2. **Where does the story take place?**

   _____

   _____

   _____

3. **List the characters in the story.**

   _____

   _____

   _____

4. **Name the problem(s) Gabe encounters in the story.**

   _____

   _____

   _____

5. **How do you predict the problem will be solved? Underline the details that helped you decide this.**

   _____

   _____

   _____

English/
Language Arts

ELA4R1

Identifying
the Speaker

DIRECTIONS: Read the passages and then answer the questions.

Samantha's Birthday

A. I knew it would be a great day from the minute I woke up. Piled beside my bed was a stack of presents. I jumped out of bed. I was so excited. When I came downstairs carrying the presents, everyone shouted, "Happy birthday!"

B. Before Samantha woke up, I left her presents beside her bed. I knew she would like the surprise from her father and me. When we saw Samantha on the stairs, we surprised her by saying, "Happy birthday!"

C. I bought Samantha a book about dinosaurs for her birthday. Mom and Dad let me do extra chores to earn the money. I had to wake up early to surprise her, but it was worth it to see her face when we all said, "Happy birthday!"

1. Who is the speaker in passage A?

_____

What special day is it for this person?

_____

2. Who is the speaker in passage B?

_____

How did you guess?

_____

3. Who is the speaker in passage C?

_____

How did you guess?

_____

4. All of these passages are written from what point of view?

(A) first person

(B) second person

(C) third person

(D) none of these

**English/
Language Arts**
ELA4R1

Identifying Figurative
Language and Foreshadowing

DIRECTIONS: Read the passage and answer the questions on the next page.

Sollie, the Rock

I've lived on a lake for most of my life. I've had lots of time to learn all sorts of fun things to do in the water. I think my favorite thing of all is water skiing. That's why I decided to invite my best friend, Sollie, over to give it a try.

Sollie had never been on skis before, but I knew Dad could help him learn, just like he helped me.

Water skiing is like flying. If you aren't afraid of getting up, you'll enjoy the ride. That's what I told Sollie before we spent the afternoon trying to get him up on skis for the first time.

I thought it would be easy. Sollie is a seal, sleek and smooth in the water, bobbing in and out of the waves. I thought someone so agile would find skiing easy. It didn't dawn on me until the fourth try that Sollie is shaped more like a rock than a bird.

On his first try, Sollie let go of the towrope when Dad hit the gas. He sank as fast as the *Titanic*. The only things visible were the tips of his skis.

On his second try, Sollie leaned into the skis, flipping head over heels like a gymnast falling off the balance beam. His skis formed an "X" that marked the spot where he disappeared.

On the third try, Sollie stood up. He teetered forward and then back, as if he were a rag doll. His biggest mistake was holding on to the rope after he lost both skis. He flopped about behind the boat like a giant carp until he finally let go.

On the fourth try, Sollie bent his knees, straightened his back, and flew around the lake behind the boat as if he were a professional skier. He jumped the wake, rolled out next to the boat, and waved at me. He was "the man."

After three times around the lake, Sollie let go of the rope. He returned to his former self and dropped into the water like a rock.

After spending the afternoon out on the water with Dad and me, Sollie fell in love with water skiing. We made plans to do it again soon. Maybe even a rock can learn to fly!

Metaphor—a direct comparison between unlike things. Example: Bobby is a mouse.

Simile—an indirect comparison between two unlike things using the words *like, as,* or *as if* to make the comparison. Example: Bobby is like a mouse.

Alliteration—the use of words that repeat the same beginning sound. Example: Round and round the rugged rock the ragged rascal ran.

1. **Identify the following lines as metaphors (M) or similes (S).**

   _____ Sollie is a seal, sleek and smooth in the water, bobbing in and out of the waves.

   _____ Sollie is shaped more like a rock than a bird.

   _____ He sank as fast as the *Titanic.*

   _____ He flopped about behind the boat like a giant carp until he finally let go.

2. **What do the above similes suggest about Sollie?**

   _____

   _____

   _____

   _____

3. **Why is the following sentence not a simile or a metaphor?**

   Sollie bent his knees, straightened his back, and flew around the lake behind the boat as if he were a professional skier.

   (A) It does not make a comparison.

   (B) It makes a comparison between like things.

   (C) It makes a contrast rather than a comparison.

   (D) The comparison is not between a person and an animal.

4. **Fill in the blank to turn the sentence into a simile.**

   Sollie bent his knees, straightened his back, and flew around the lake behind the boat . . .

   _____

   _____

   _____ .

5. **Identify the use of alliteration given in the fourth paragraph of the story.**

   _____

   _____

   _____

   _____

6. **Foreshadowing means to indicate that something is going to happen—and it is usually something unpleasant. Which of the following sentences is an example of foreshadowing?**

   (F) Water skiing is like flying.

   (G) We made plans to do it again soon.

   (H) I thought it would be easy.

   (J) After spending the afternoon out on the water with me and Dad, Sollie fell in love with water skiiing.

STOP

English/
Language Arts

ELA4R1

Making Inferences

DIRECTIONS: Read the story and then answer the questions.

> Cassie's mom has errands to run, so Cassie agrees to stay home to babysit for her little brother, who is asleep. Her mom also leaves Cassie a list of chores to do while she is gone. Cassie will be able to go to the mall with her friends when her chores are finished and her mom gets back. As soon as Cassie's mom leaves, Cassie starts calling her friends on the phone. She talks to Kim for 20 minutes and to Beth for 15 minutes. She is supposed to call Maria when she finishes talking to Jackie.
>
> After talking on the phone, Cassie decides to do her nails while she watches a movie on TV. After the movie, Cassie listens to the radio and reads a magazine. Before Cassie realizes it, three and a half hours have passed and her mom is back home. Her mom walks in and finds the kitchen still a mess, crumbs all over the carpet, dusty furniture, and Cassie's little brother screaming in his room.

1. What is the setting for this story?

- (A) the mall
- (B) Cassie's house
- (C) Jackie's house
- (D) the kitchen

2. What do we know about the main character?

- (F) She has errands to run.
- (G) She has chores to do.
- (H) He is asleep.
- (J) He is screaming in his room.

3. What is the plot of this story?

- (A) Cassie must do her chores if she wants to go to the mall. But she wastes the time instead.
- (B) Cassie's mother has errands to run. She leaves Cassie in charge of the house.
- (C) Cassie's brother is asleep in his room. He wakes up screaming.
- (D) Cassie is grounded.

4. Which of the following is a task Cassie probably wasn't supposed to do?

- (F) dust
- (G) listen for her brother
- (H) do her nails
- (J) clean the kitchen

5. What do you think the resolution to this problem will be?

- (A) Cassie's little brother will have to do all the chores.
- (B) Cassie will be punished and will not go to the mall.
- (C) Cassie's mom will drive her to the mall.
- (D) Cassie, her mom, and her brother will go to a movie.

STOP

ELA4R1

Identifying
Themes or Lessons

DIRECTIONS: Read the passages and then answer the questions.

Walks All Over the Sky

Back when the sky was completely dark there was a chief with two sons, a younger son, One Who Walks All Over the Sky, and an older son, Walking About Early. The younger son was sad to see the sky always so dark so he made a mask out of wood and pitch (the Sun) and lit it on fire. Each day he travels across the sky. At night he sleeps below the horizon and when he snores sparks fly from the mask and make the stars. The older brother became jealous. To impress their father he smeared fat and charcoal on his face (the Moon) and makes his own path across the sky.

—From the *Tsimshian of the Pacific Northwest*

1. **This passage is which genre (type) of literature**
   - (A) folktale
   - (B) nonfiction
   - (C) poetry
   - (D) fable

2. **What is the theme of this story?**

   _____

   _____

   _____

   _____

   _____

Fox and the Grapes

One warm summer day, a fox was walking along when he noticed a bunch of grapes on a vine above him. Cool, juicy grapes would taste so good. The more he thought about it, the more the fox wanted those grapes. He tried standing on his tiptoes. He tried jumping high in the air. He tried getting a running start before he jumped. But no matter what he tried, the fox could not reach the grapes. As he angrily walked away, the fox muttered, "They were probably sour anyway!"

Moral: A person (or fox) sometimes pretends that he does not want something that he or she cannot have.

3. **This passage is which genre (type) of literature?**
   - (F) poetry
   - (G) folktale
   - (H) nonfiction
   - (J) fable

4. **What is the lesson, or moral, of this story?**

   _____

   _____

   _____

   _____

   _____

STOP

English/
Language Arts   **Interpreting Poetry**   Readin

ELA4R1

DIRECTIONS: Read the poem and then answer the questions.

Sunset

At the end of the day
Sank the sun in the sky.
The colors were children,
Alive and bright-eyed.

The lake was the glass
Reflecting their play.
How gorgeous this close,
This end to the day.

The clouds were the pillows
For each child to rest,
Ready to sleep
Now so colorfully dressed.

1. In this poem, the clouds are compared to

   _____

2. The colors of the sunset are compared to

   _____

   in the poem.

3. How many verses are in this poem?

   _____

4. In the second verse, which words rhyme?

   _____

   _____

5. In each of the verses, which lines rhyme?

   _____

   _____

   _____

6. Each verse has a rhythm, or pattern, as it is
   read. The rhythm is identified by the number
   of syllables in each line. For the first verse,
   identify the number of syllables in each line.
   The first one is done for you.

   Line 1 _____6_____

   Line 2 _____

   Line 3 _____

   Line 4 _____

**English/
Language Arts**

| ELA4R1 |

Identifying
Textual Features

DIRECTIONS: Read the passage and answer the questions that follow.

The Origins of the Telegraph

Have you ever watched someone tap a key and send a code for SOS? Perhaps you have seen an old film showing a ship about to sink. Perhaps someone was tapping wildly on a device, trying to send for help.

From where did this system of tapping out dashes and dots come? Who invented this electronic device? Samuel Morse invented the telegraph and the electronic alphabet called *Morse code.*

When Morse was young, he was an artist. People in New York knew his work well and liked it a great deal. Being well known, Morse decided to run for office. He ran for the office of New York mayor and congressman, but he lost these political races.

In 1832, while Morse was sailing back to the United States from Europe, he thought of an electronic telegraph. This would help people communicate across great distances, even from ship to shore. He was anxious to put together his invention as quickly as possible. Interestingly, someone else had also thought of this same idea.

By 1835, he had put together his first telegraph, but it was only experimental. In 1844, he built a telegraph line from Baltimore to Washington, D.C. He later made his telegraph better, and in 1849, was granted a patent by the U.S. government. Within a few years, people communicated across 23,000 miles of telegraph wire.

As a result of Samuel Morse's invention, trains ran more safely. Conductors could warn about dangers or problems across great distances and ask for help. People in business could communicate more easily, which made it easier to sell their goods and services. Morse had changed communication forever.

---

1. **How many paragraphs are in this passage?**

   (A) 3   (C) 5

   (B) 4   (D) 6

2. **What is the main idea of this passage?**

   (F) Samuel Morse was an artist.

   (G) Samuel Morse invented the telegraph, which became an important tool for communication.

   (H) Samuel Morse wanted to help people communicate across great distances.

   (J) Ships use a code known as SOS when they need help.

3. **Which sentence is the topic sentence for paragraph 4?**

   (A) sentence 1   (C) sentence 3

   (B) sentence 2   (D) sentence 4

4. **Which sentence is the concluding sentence for the passage?**

   (F) Being well known, Morse decided to run for office.

   (G) Morse had changed communication forever.

   (H) Within a few years, people communicated across 23,000 miles of telegraph wire.

   (J) When Morse was young, he was an artist.

English/
Language Arts

ELA4R1

Using Charts

DIRECTIONS: Read the passage, and then fill in the chart below to compare the Fahrenheit and Celsius scales.

Temperature Rising

Can you imagine a hot summer day with a temperature of 30 degrees? Or having a fever of 38 degrees that sends you to the doctor? If you're thinking in degrees Fahrenheit, you're probably confused. Another way to measure temperature is in degrees Celsius. The temperature scales on most thermometers show both Fahrenheit and Celsius.

An early version of a thermometer was made in 1593. Gabriel Fahrenheit invented the first mercury thermometer in 1714. The Fahrenheit scale is named after him. On the Fahrenheit scale, water freezes at 32°F, water boils at 212°F, and normal body temperature is 98.6°F.

Anders Celsius was a Swedish astronomer born in 1701. He experimented with a scale based on 100 degrees. On the Celsius scale, water freezes at 0°C, water boils at 100°C, and normal body temperature is 37°C.

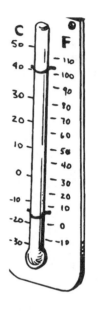

Facts	Fahrenheit	Celsius
Invented by		
Water freezes		
Normal body temperature		
Water boils		

ELA4R1

Summarizing Main Ideas and Supporting Details

DIRECTIONS: Read the passage and answer the questions.

Sound

It is easy to take sounds for granted. But do you really know what sound is? Sound is caused by something quivering back and forth. This shaking motion is called a *vibration.* Vibrations travel through the air and you hear them as sounds. You can hear many sounds at the same time because the air can carry many vibrations at one time. Different sounds are created according to how fast something vibrates. The faster it vibrates, the higher the sound. A slower vibration causes a lower sound.

Unpleasant sounds are called *noise.* Some noise can be harmful to your hearing. Loud noises, such as those from airplanes or machines, can even cause a hearing loss. But other sounds, such as music or talking, are not dangerous—just pleasant.

1. **The main idea of this passage is about _____ .**
   - (A) sound
   - (B) vibration
   - (C) noise
   - (D) hearing loss

2. **Noise, as discussed in this passage, is _____ .**
   - (F) pleasant
   - (G) a secondary idea
   - (H) not dangerous
   - (J) the main idea

3. **Sound is caused by _____ .**
   - (A) music and talking
   - (B) vibrations in the air
   - (C) airplanes and machines
   - (D) the air carrying noise

4. **Faster vibrations _____ .**
   - (F) never cause hearing loss
   - (G) always cause unpleasant sounds
   - (H) cause higher sounds
   - (J) travel through the air several at a time

5. **Different sounds are made _____ .**
   - (A) by your hearing
   - (B) according to how hot the air becomes
   - (C) according to how noisy something is
   - (D) according to how fast something vibrates

19

English/
Language Arts

ELA4R1

Distinguishing Fact and Opinion

Reading

DIRECTIONS: Read the passage and answer the questions that follow.

Stonehenge is an ancient monument made up of a group of huge stones. It is located in Wiltshire, England. No one knows who put the stones there or what they are for. Some scientists think that they were put there thousands of years ago by people who worshiped the sun.

Through the years, many of the original stones have fallen or have been carried away and used to build other things. But many stones still stand in place. From these stones and other markings, scientists think they know how the monument looked when it was first built. Some think that Stonehenge was built by ancient people to study the sun. These people may have used the monument to predict changes in the seasons—even eclipses of the sun. Today, Stonehenge is one of the most popular tourist stops in England.

1. **Which of the following is a fact about Stonehenge?**

   (A) Scientists know what Stonehenge looked like when it was first built.

   (B) Stonehenge is located in Wiltshire, England.

   (C) Scientists know why Stonehenge was built.

   (D) Stonehenge helped people study eclipses of the sun.

2. **Which of the following is an opinion about Stonehenge?**

   (F) Some of the stones were carried away.

   (G) Stonehenge is in England.

   (H) The stones are in a circle.

   (J) Stonehenge is the most popular tourist stop in England.

3. **Write *F* if the statement is false and *T* if it is true.**

   _____ Over the years, many stones have fallen or were carried away.

   _____ Only five stones remain as a monument.

   _____ Ancient people may have used the monument to study the sun.

   _____ Stonehenge was built ten years ago.

Name _____   Date _____

DIRECTIONS: Read the passage and answer the questions that follow.

A Bumpy Ride

When we first climbed into the car and strapped on our safety belts, I wasn't very nervous. I was sitting right next to my big brother, and he had done this many times before. As we started to climb the hill, however, I could feel my heart jump into my throat.

"Brian?" I asked nervously. "Is this supposed to be so noisy?"

"Sure, Matthew," Brian answered. "It always does that."

A minute later, we whooshed so fast down the hill I didn't have time to think. With a twist, a loop, and a bunch of fast turns, everyone on board screamed in delight. No wonder this was one of the most popular rides in the park. By the time the car pulled into the station and we got off the ride, I was ready to do it again!

1. **Which of the following best describes the setting of this story?**

   (A) a car ride to school

   (B) a train ride

   ● a ride on a roller coaster

   (D) a trip to the grocery store

2. **From the beginning to end of this story, Matthew went from being _____ .**

   ● nervous to calm to scared

   (G) calm to nervous to bored

   (H) bored to excited to scared

   (J) calm to nervous to excited

3. **What might have happened if this story had taken place in a regular car?**

   (A) Brian might have lost his license for careless driving.

   (B) Brian might have started a taxi business.

   (C) Matthew might have wanted to drive with Brian again.

   ● Matthew might not have been nervous.

DIRECTIONS: Read the passage and answer the questions that follow.

Corey went zooming to the park to meet his buddies for an afternoon of hoops. It would have been a perfect day, but he had to drag his little brother Pete along.

"Wait for me, Corey," whined Pete.

Corey walked Pete over to a nearby tree, handed him his lunch, and said, "Sit here and eat. Don't move until I come back and get you." Corey ran off to meet his buddies.

As Pete began eating, he heard the pitter-patter of rain falling around him. When Pete saw lightning, he ran for shelter. Suddenly, a loud crack of lightning sounded. Looking behind him, Pete saw the top of the tree come crashing down right where he had been sitting. Corey saw it too, from the other side of the park.

"Pete!" Corey screamed as he ran. At the moment the lightning struck, Corey thought, "Pete's not the drag I always thought he was."

4. What is the main conflict in this story?

- ● Corey has to drag his brother along to the park.
- (G) There is a lightning storm.
- (H) The tree crashes down.
- (J) Corey thinks Pete is hurt.

5. This passage is written from what point of view?

- ● first person
- (B) second person
- (C) third person
- (D) none of these

6. Why does Corey realize that Pete is not such a drag?

- (F) They have fun together.
- (G) He didn't have to save him.
- (H) Pete turns out to be a great runner.
- ● He realizes that he had been taking his little brother for granted.

DIRECTIONS: Read the passage and answer the questions that follow.

During the 1700s, America wanted to gain independence from the British. This caused many struggles between the two countries.

The British passed a law in 1765 that required legal papers and other items to have a tax stamp. It was called the Stamp Act. Colonists were forced to pay a fee for the stamp. Secret groups began to work against the requirement of the tax stamp. The law was finally taken away in 1766.

In 1767, the British passed the Townshend Acts. These acts forced people to pay fees for many items, such as tea, paper, glass, lead, and paint. This wasn't fair.

Colonists were furious. On December 16, 1773, they tossed 342 chests of tea over the sides of ships in Boston Harbor. This was later called the Boston Tea Party. Colonists had shown that they would not accept these laws.

7. Which of the following sentences from the story states an opinion?

- (A) The British passed a law in 1765 that required legal papers and other items to have a tax stamp.
- (B) The law was finally taken away in 1766.
- (C) This was later called the Boston Tea Party.
- ● This wasn't fair.

8. What caused the colonists to throw 342 chests of tea into Boston Harbor?

- ● They were angry about the Townshend Acts.
- (G) They wanted to make a big pot of tea.
- (H) The tea was bad.
- (J) They were angry because of the Stamp Act.

9. In what year did the Boston Tea Party occur?

- (A) 1767
- (B) 1765
- ● 1773
- (D) 1766

10. What is the main idea of this passage?

- (F) Colonists did not want the tax stamp.
- (G) The colonists' desire for independence caused conflict with the British.
- (H) Colonists showed they would not accept British laws.
- ● The British passed an act that forced the colonists to pay a fee for items.

STOP

Reading Standards

Reading Standards ELA4R1 and ELA4R2 *(See pages 6–7.)*

ELA4R3. The student understands and acquires new vocabulary and uses it correctly in reading and writing. *(See pages 25–29.)* The student:
a. reads a variety of texts and incorporates new words into oral and written language.
b. determines the meaning of unknown words using their context.
c. identifies the meaning of common root words to determine the meaning of unfamiliar words.
d. determines meanings of words and alternate word choices using a dictionary or thesaurus.
e. identifies the meaning of common prefixes (e.g., un-, re-, dis-).
f. identifies the meaning of common idioms and figurative phrases.
g. identifies playful uses of language (e.g., puns, jokes, palindromes).
h. recognizes and uses words with multiple meanings (e.g., sentence, school, hard) and determines which meaning is intended from the context of the sentence.
i. identifies and applies the meaning of the terms antonym, synonym, and homophone.

What it means:
● Students should be able to use different strategies to help them determine the meaning of unfamiliar words.
● Students should know that **figurative language** is language used for descriptive effect. It describes or implies meaning, rather than directly stating it. Examples of figurative language include similes, metaphors, hyperbole, and personification.
● Students should know that an **idiom** is an expression or saying that states one thing but means another.
● Students should be able to identify the multiple meanings of words. For example, they should know that *bill* can mean the "beak of a bird" or "a monthly expense."
● Students should be able to identify **synonyms** (words that mean the same), **antonyms** (words with opposite meanings), and **homophones** (words that sound alike but have different meanings and spellings).

ELA4R4. The student reads aloud, accurately (in the range of 95%), familiar material in a variety of genres of the quality and complexity illustrated in the sample reading list, in a way that makes meaning clear to listeners. *(See pages 30–31.)* The student:
a. uses letter-sound knowledge to decode written English and uses a range of cueing systems (e.g., phonics and context clues) to determine pronunciation and meaning.
b. uses self-correction when subsequent reading indicates an earlier miscue (self-monitoring and self-correcting strategies).
c. reads with a rhythm, flow, and meter that sounds like everyday speech (prosody).

Reading Standards

Grade Four Reading List

This is a sample reading list from which the students and teachers could select. This list is not exclusive. Acceptable titles also appear on lists produced by organizations such as the National Council of Teachers of English and the American Library Association. Substitutions might also be made from lists approved locally.

Fiction

Atwater, *Mr. Popper's Penguins*
Avi, *No More Magic*
Blume, *Fudge-a-Mania*
Blume, *Tales of a Fourth Grade Nothing*
Byars, *Midnight Fox*
Clements, *Frindle*
Dalgliesh, *The Courage of Sarah Noble*
Dahl, *Charlie and the Chocolate Factory*
Dahl, *James and the Giant Peach*
Fritz, *The Cabin Faced West*
Gardiner, *Stone Fox*
MacLachlan, *Sarah, Plain and Tall*
Mohr, *Felita*
Naylor, *Shiloh*
Sachar, *There's a Boy in the Girls' Bathroom*
Smith, *Taste of Blackberries*
White, *Charlotte's Web*
White, *The Trumpet and the Swan*

Nonfiction

Anderson, *Pioneer Girl: The Story of Laura Ingalls Wilder*
Cherry, *The Great Kapok Tree*
Fritz, *And Then What Happened, Paul Revere?*
Fritz, *Shh! We're Writing the Constitution*
George, *One Day in the Alpine Tundra*
Graff, *Helen Keller: Crusader for the Blind and Deaf*
Norrell, *We Want Jobs: Story of the Great Depression*
Slaughter, *Exploring with Lewis and Clark: Reflections on Men and Wilderness*
Weldon, *Exploring Space*

Poetry

Greenfield, *Honey, I Love* and *Other Love Poems*
De Regniers, Moore, White, and Carr, eds., *Sing a Song of Popcorn*
Silverstein, *Where the Sidewalk Ends*

English/
Language Arts

Reading

Identifying Root Words

ELA4R3

DIRECTIONS: Choose the correct definition for the root in each word.

Example:

In the word *candle*, *cand* means _____ .

- (A) erase
- (B) dark
- (C) glow
- (D) invisible

Answer: (C)

1. In the word *abbreviate*, *brev* means

_____ .

- (A) to lengthen
- (B) to shorten
- (C) to make a list
- (D) to learn how to spell

2. In the word *autograph*, *graph* means

_____ .

- (F) to read
- (G) to draw a picture
- (H) to write
- (J) to measure something

3. In the word *telescope*, *tele* means _____ .

- (A) empty space
- (B) far away
- (C) close up
- (D) temperature

4. In the word *geography*, *geo* means

_____ .

- (F) stars
- (G) Earth
- (H) the human body
- (J) insects

5. In the word *triangle*, *tri* means _____ .

- (A) one
- (B) two
- (C) three
- (D) four

6. In the word *bicycle*, *cycl* means _____ .

- (F) wheel
- (G) handlebars
- (H) spokes
- (J) chain

7. In the word *action*, *ac* means _____ .

- (A) eat
- (B) fill
- (C) subtract
- (D) do

8. In the word *autobiography*, *auto* means

_____ .

- (F) car
- (G) friendly
- (H) self
- (J) television

STOP

English/
Language Arts

ELA4R3

Using Resources

Clue

Remember, dictionary entries can tell you more than just the meaning of a word. They can also help you say a word correctly and tell you if a word is a noun, verb, adjective, adverb, or pronoun.

DIRECTIONS: Use the dictionary entries to answer questions 1–3.

save [sāv] *v.* **1.** to rescue from harm or danger **2.** to keep in a safe condition **3.** to set aside for future use; store **4.** to avoid

saving [sā´vĭng] *n.* **1.** rescuing from harm or danger **2.** avoiding excess spending; economy **3.** something saved

savory [sā´və-rē] *adj.* **1.** appealing to the taste or smell **2.** salty to the taste

1. **The *a* in the word *saving* sounds most like the word _____ .**
   - (A) pat
   - (B) ape
   - (C) heated
   - (D) naughty

2. **Which sentence uses *save* in the same way as definition number 3?**
   - (F) Firefighters save lives.
   - (G) She saves half of all she earns.
   - (H) Going by jet saves eight hours of driving.
   - (J) The life jacket saved the boy from drowning.

3. **Which sentence uses *savory* in the same way as definition number 2?**
   - (A) The savory stew made me thirsty.
   - (B) The savory bank opened an account.
   - (C) This flower has a savory scent.
   - (D) The savory dog rescued me.

DIRECTIONS: Use the sample thesaurus to answer questions 4–6.

head [hed] *n.* **1.** skull, scalp, *noggin **2.** leader, commander, director, chief, manager **3.** top, summit, peak **4.** front **5.** toilet, restroom (on a boat) **6.** come to a head, reach the end or turning point **7.** heads up watch out, duck, be careful **8.** keep one's head, stay calm, *roll with the punches

head [hed] *v.* **1.** lead, command, direct, supervise

Key: *adj.* adjective, *adv.* adverb, *n.* noun, *v.* verb, *slang

4. **"Noggin" and "roll with the punches" are both examples of**
   - (F) verbs
   - (G) nouns
   - (H) slang
   - (J) adjectives

5. **How is the underlined word used in this sentence?**
   She was chosen to <u>head</u> the Art Club.
   - (A) noun
   - (B) adverb
   - (C) slang
   - (D) verb

6. **What would be another way to say, "Watch out!"?**
   - (F) keep your head
   - (G) come to a head
   - (H) heads up
   - (J) roll with the punches

Name _____   Date _____

Identifying
Common Prefixes

DIRECTIONS: Choose a prefix from the Prefix Bank and add it to the root word to make a new word. Then use the new word in a sentence.

Prefix Bank

Prefix	Meaning
anti-	against
be-	cause to be
co-	with or together
dis-	not or without
pre-	before
pro-	in place of
re-	again
un-	not

Clue A prefix is a word part that when added to a root word changes the word's meaning.

1. _____ + view = "to see before"

_____

_____

2. _____ + happy = "not happy"

_____

_____

3. _____ + little = "to cause to feel small"

_____

_____

4. _____ + workers = "people one works with"

_____

_____

5. _____ + trust = "without trust"

_____

_____

6. _____ + play = "to play again"

_____

_____

STOP

English/
Language Arts

ELA4R3

Synonyms and Antonyms

DIRECTIONS: Read each item. Choose the word that means the same or about the same as the underlined word.

1. attend a <u>conference</u>
   - (A) party
   - (B) game
   - (C) meeting
   - (D) race

2. <u>beautiful</u> painting
   - (F) pretty
   - (G) interesting
   - (H) colorful
   - (J) light

3. <u>repair</u> the car
   - (A) clean
   - (B) drive
   - (C) fix
   - (D) sell

4. <u>thin</u> slice
   - (F) short
   - (G) skinny
   - (H) long
   - (J) wide

5. To <u>rush</u> through your homework is to _____ .
   - (A) relax
   - (B) slow
   - (C) finish
   - (D) hurry

DIRECTIONS: Read each item. Choose the word that means the opposite of the underlined word.

6. Banana slugs are <u>moist</u> to the touch.
   - (F) dry
   - (G) slimy
   - (H) rough
   - (J) rubbery

7. The dog's fur felt <u>silky</u>.
   - (A) soft
   - (B) smooth
   - (C) rough
   - (D) dirty

8. <u>docile</u> animal
   - (F) vicious
   - (G) gentle
   - (H) shy
   - (J) quiet

9. <u>active</u> child
   - (A) immobile
   - (B) exhausted
   - (C) bored
   - (D) thrilled

10. left <u>promptly</u>
    - (F) late
    - (G) recently
    - (H) quietly
    - (J) slowly

28

English/
Language Arts

ELA4R3

Using Homophones

Clue

A **homophone** is a word that sounds like another word but has a different meaning and spelling. For example, *throne* and *thrown* are homophones.

DIRECTIONS: Write the homophone for each of the following words.

1. plain   _____

2. right   _____

3. see   _____

4. knew   _____

5. here   _____

6. for   _____

7. no   _____

8. be   _____

9. witch   _____

DIRECTIONS: Fill in the blanks with the correct form of *to, too,* or *two.*

10. **Brad and Trisha went _____ the store and looked at video games.**

11. **Brad saw _____ video games he wanted to buy.**

12. **"I've played those games _____ ," Trish said.**

13. **"I'd like to buy them, but I think they will cost _____ much," Brad said.**

14. **They went _____ look at other games and compare the prices.**

DIRECTIONS: Fill in the blanks with the correct form of *there, their,* or *they're.*

15. **Nancy and Sue are feeding _____ pets.**

16. **_____ feeding the ducks, rabbits, and geese first.**

17. **"Nancy, would you carry this bag of food over _____ ?" asked Sue.**

18. **"I will carry it over _____ if you will watch that the rabbits don't run out of _____ cage," said Sue.**

19. **" _____ gone!" shouted Nancy.**

20. **The girls looked and saw _____ pet rabbits running off behind the bushes.**

STOP

Using
Decoding Strategies

DIRECTIONS: Find the word that means the same as the underlined word.

1. Tara's <u>excuse</u> was a good one.
Excuse means _____ .

- (A) dismiss
- (B) forgive
- (C) explanation
- (D) forgotten

2. The dog seemed <u>fearless</u> as it raced into the crashing waves.
Fearless means _____ .

- (F) happy
- (G) sincere
- (H) angry
- (J) unafraid

3. The house was heated by <u>solar</u> energy.
Solar means _____ .

- (A) electric
- (B) water
- (C) sun-powered
- (D) gas

4. The roofer used an <u>extension</u> ladder to fix the shingles.
Extension means _____ .

- (F) rolling
- (G) expandable
- (H) heavy
- (J) permanent

DIRECTIONS: Find the sentence which uses the underlined word in the same way.

5. The <u>field</u> is planted with corn.

- (A) The field of technology is constantly changing.
- (B) We can see deer in the field by our house.
- (C) Her field is nursing.
- (D) Our field trip is next Thursday.

6. The <u>general</u> idea was to weave a basket.

- (F) She is a general in the army.
- (G) The soldiers followed their general into battle.
- (H) I think that the general had the best idea.
- (J) No general study of history can cover everything.

7. Brake pads are made at a <u>plant</u> in our city.

- (A) The most beautiful plant is a rose.
- (B) Plant your feet and don't move.
- (C) Farmers plant crops.
- (D) My uncle worked at the plant.

STOP

**English/
Language Arts**

ELA4R4

Determining Meaning Using Content

DIRECTIONS: Read the passage. Then answer the questions that follow.

Snakes

How much do you know about snakes? Read these snake facts and find out.

- A snake skeleton has numerous ribs. A large snake may have as many as 400 pairs!
- Most snakes have poor eyesight. They track other animals by sensing their body heat.
- Snakes can't blink! They sleep with their eyes open.
- Although all snakes have teeth, very few of them—only the venomous ones—have fangs.
- Many snakes are very docile and unlikely to bite people.
- Pet snakes recognize their owners by smell. They flick their tongues in the air to detect smells.
- Snakes have special ways of hearing. Sound vibrations from the earth pass through their bellies to receptors in their spines. Airborne sounds pass through snakes' lungs to receptors in their skin.

1. *Numerous* means about the same as

    _____ .

    (A) number
    (B) many
    (C) few
    (D) special

2. **In this passage,** *poor* **means the opposite of** _____ .

    (F) rich
    (G) good
    (H) happy
    (J) broke

3. **What does** *track* **mean as it is used in this passage?**

    (A) the rails on which a train moves
    (B) a sport that includes running, jumping, and throwing
    (C) to follow the footprints of
    (D) to find and follow

4. **What does the word** *venomous* **mean as it is used in this passage?**

    (F) vicious
    (G) sharp
    (H) poisonous
    (J) huge

5. **Which word means the opposite of** *docile*?

    (A) vicious
    (B) shy
    (C) gentle
    (D) active

6. **Which word means the same as** *detect*?

    (F) enjoy
    (G) arrest
    (H) find
    (J) hide

7. **A receptor** _____ **something.**

    (A) throws
    (B) takes in
    (C) gives
    (D) sees

8. **Airborne sounds are** _____ .

    (F) carried through the air
    (G) carried through the earth
    (H) always made by wind
    (J) louder than other sounds

STOP

English/
Language Arts

ELA4R3–ELA4R4

For pages 25–31

Mini-Test 2

DIRECTIONS: Choose the best answer.

1. **Which of these words probably comes from the Greek word *logos,* meaning *word* or *speech?***

   Ⓐ locate

   Ⓑ logo

   Ⓒ lodge

   Ⓓ log

2. **Let's _____ the ripe apples.**

   Which word means *to gather* the ripe apples?

   Ⓕ eat

   Ⓖ collect

   Ⓗ check

   Ⓙ sell

3. **Find the sentence in which the underlined word is used in the same way.**

   The <u>field</u> is planted with corn.

   Ⓐ The field of technology is always changing.

   Ⓑ We can see deer in the field by our house.

   Ⓒ Her field is nursing.

   Ⓓ Our field trip is next Thursday.

4. **Which answer best defines the prefix?**

   <u>mis</u>take   <u>mis</u>lead

   Ⓕ correctly

   Ⓖ before

   Ⓗ to do after

   Ⓙ wrongly

5. **Which word means the same or about the same as the underlined word?**

   <u>fearless</u> dog

   Ⓐ careless

   Ⓑ energetic

   Ⓒ unafraid

   Ⓓ sincere

6. **Which word means the opposite of the underlined word?**

   <u>dishonest</u> advertisement

   Ⓕ trustworthy

   Ⓖ imaginary

   Ⓗ true

   Ⓙ false

DIRECTIONS: Read the passage, and then answer the question.

A Microscope

Have you ever looked into a microscope? A microscope is an instrument that helps us see very small things by magnifying them. Scientists and doctors can use microscopes to study parts of the body, such as blood and skin cells. They can also study germs, tiny plants, and tiny animals.

7. **In this passage, what does the word *magnifying* mean?**

   Ⓐ making them smaller

   Ⓑ making them larger

   Ⓒ making them red

   Ⓓ making them disappear

Writing Standards

The student writes clear, coherent text that develops a central idea or tells a story. The writing shows consideration of the audience and purpose. The student progresses through the stages of the writing process (e.g., prewriting, drafting, revising, and editing successive versions).

ELA4W1. The student produces writing that establishes an appropriate organizational structure, sets a context and engages the reader, maintains a coherent focus throughout, and signals a satisfying closure. *(See page 35.)* The student:
a. selects a focus, an organizational structure, and a point of view based on purpose, genre expectations, audience, length, and format requirements.
b. writes texts of an appropriate length to address the topic or tell the story.
c. uses traditional structures for conveying information (e.g., chronological order, cause and effect, similarity and difference, and posing and answering a question).
d. uses appropriate structures to ensure coherence (e.g., transition elements).

ELA4W2. The student demonstrates competence in a variety of genres. *(See pages 36–39.)*
The student produces a narrative that:
a. engages the reader by establishing a context, creating a point of view, and otherwise developing reader interest.
b. establishes a plot, setting, and conflict, and/or the significance of events.
c. creates an organizational structure.
d. includes sensory details and concrete language to develop plot and character.
e. excludes extraneous details and inconsistencies.
f. develops complex characters through actions describing the motivation of characters and character conversation.
g. uses a range of appropriate narrative strategies such as dialogue, tension, or suspense.
h. provides a sense of closure to the writing.

What it means:
- Students should be able to write a story about a familiar event. Narratives typically answer the question, "What happened?"

The student produces informational writing (e.g., report, procedures, correspondence) that:
a. engages the reader by establishing a context, creating a speaker's voice, and otherwise developing reader interest.
b. frames a central question about an issue or situation.
c. creates an organizing structure appropriate to a specific purpose, audience, and context.
d. includes appropriate facts and details.
e. excludes extraneous details and inappropriate information.
f. uses a range of appropriate strategies, such as providing facts and details, describing or analyzing the subject, and narrating a relevant anecdote.
g. draws from more than one source of information such as speakers, books, newspapers, and online materials.
h. provides a sense of closure to the writing.

Writing Standards

The student produces a <u>response to literature</u> that:
a. engages the reader by establishing a context, creating a speaker's voice, and otherwise developing reader interest.
b. advances a judgment that is interpretive, evaluative, or reflective.
c. supports judgments through references to the text, other works, authors, or nonprint media, or references to personal knowledge.
d. demonstrates an understanding of the literary work (e.g., a summary that contains the main idea and most significant details of the reading selection).
e. excludes extraneous details and inappropriate information.
f. provides a sense of closure to the writing.

The student produces a <u>persuasive essay</u> that:
a. engages the reader by establishing a context, creating a speaker's voice, and otherwise developing reader interest.
b. states a clear position.
c. supports a position with relevant evidence.
d. excludes extraneous details and inappropriate information.
e. creates an organizing structure appropriate to a specific purpose, audience, and context.
f. provides a sense of closure to the writing.

ELA4W3. The student uses research and technology to support writing. *(See pages 40–41.)* The student:
a. acknowledges information from sources.
b. locates information in reference texts by using organizational features (e.g., prefaces, appendices).
c. uses various reference materials (e.g., dictionary, thesaurus, encyclopedia, electronic information) as aids to writing.
d. demonstrates basic keyboarding skills and familiarity with computer terminology (e.g., software, memory, disk drive, hard drive).

ELA4W4. The student consistently uses a writing process to develop, revise, and evaluate writing. *(See pages 42–44.)* The student:
a. plans and drafts independently and resourcefully.
b. revises selected drafts to improve coherence and progression by adding, deleting, consolidating, and rearranging text.
c. edits to correct errors in spelling, punctuation, etc.

**English/
Language Arts**

Writing

Using an Organizational Structure

ELA4W1

DIRECTIONS: Study the outline and answer the questions that follow.

Owls

I. _____

    A. Great Horned Owl

    B. Snowy Owl

    C. Barn Owl

II. **Body Characteristics**

    A. Size

    B. Body Covering

    C. _____

    D. Eyes, Talons, and Beaks

III. **Eating Habits**

    A. Mice

    B. Other Small Rodents

1. **Which of the following fits best in the blank next to I.?**

    (A) Owl Migration

    (B) Owl Habitats

    (C) Types of Owls

    (D) Owl Eating Habits

2. **Which of the following fits best in the blank next to C.?**

    (F) Feather Variations

    (G) Grasses and Leaves

    (H) Trees

    (J) Nocturnal

3. **Explain how the organization of the outline makes it easier to understand the information presented.**

_____

_____

_____

_____

_____

_____

_____

_____

_____

**English/
Language Arts**

| ELA4W2 |

Writing a Narrative

DIRECTIONS: This is the beginning of a story. Read it and use your own ideas to help you finish the story.

> It was finally getting cooler. After a blazing hot day, the sun had finally gone down. Hannah still couldn't believe their car had broken down. She also couldn't believe her father had decided to walk three miles through the desert for help. The map showed a town up ahead, but they hadn't seen any cars go by for over an hour. She was alone with her mother and her sister, Abigail.

1. What problem does Hannah's family have?

_____

_____

_____

_____

_____

_____

_____

2. Describe two ways that this story might turn out.

_____

_____

_____

_____

_____

_____

_____

_____

3. What are some of the sounds, sights, and feelings that Hannah's family might have experienced?

_____

_____

_____

_____

_____

_____

_____

4. Use the details from your answers to questions 1–3 to write the ending to the story.

_____

_____

_____

_____

_____

_____

_____

_____

STOP

**English/
Language Arts**

ELA4W2

Analyzing Informational Reports

DIRECTIONS: Read the passage and answer the questions that follow.

Perhaps you have heard that many types of bats have very small eyes and do not see well. Still, as they swoop through the night, they do not bump into objects and are able to find food, even though they can't see their prey. How is this possible? Echolocation!

You might recognize the beginning of the word echolocation as echo, and you might recognize the last part of the word as location. This gives you clues about how echolocation works. The bat sends out sounds. The sounds bounce off objects and return to the bat. Echolocation not only tells the bat that objects are nearby, it also tells the bat just how far away the objects are.

Bats are not the only creatures that use echolocation. Porpoises and some types of whales and birds use it as well. It is a very effective tool for the animals that use it.

1. **What is the main idea of this passage?**

_____

_____

_____

_____

_____

2. **Why do you think the writer chose to show how the word *echolocation* can be broken into *echo* and *location*?**

_____

_____

_____

_____

3. **What are two questions that you think the writer might answer in later paragraphs?**

_____

_____

_____

_____

4. **Name some resources that you could use to find the answers to the questions you wrote in question 3.**

_____

_____

_____

_____

_____

_____

STOP

Responding to Literature

DIRECTIONS: Read the passage and then answer the questions.

The Un-Birthday

In my family, we don't celebrate birthdays. At least not like most families. My friends say I have an "un-birthday."

The tradition started with my grandmother. She and Grandfather grew up in Poland. They escaped before World War II and made their way to America. When they got here, they were so grateful that they decided to share what they had with others. On their birthdays, they gave each other just one small gift. Then they each bought a gift for someone who needed it more than they did.

As the years passed and the family grew, the tradition continued. On my last birthday, I got a backpack for school. We had a little party with cake and all of that, and then we headed off to the Lionel School for disabled kids. Some of the children were in electric wheelchairs, and only a few could walk. I picked this school because a friend has a sister there.

When we walked in with our arms full of gifts, the kids were really excited. Even though we gave them little things—like sticker books and puzzles—all the presents were wrapped and had bows.

I gave Maggie, my friend's sister, a floppy stuffed animal. Maggie can't talk, but she hugged her stuffed animal and looked at me so I knew she was grateful.

I don't get as much stuff as my friends, but it's okay, even though I want a new skateboard. Seeing Maggie and the others receive their gifts was a lot better than getting a bunch of presents myself.

---

1. **How do you think the narrator feels about this unusual family tradition?**

   _____

   _____

   _____

2. **How does the narrator know that Maggie liked her gift?**

   _____

   _____

   _____

3. **Would the narrator agree with the saying, "It is better to give than to receive"? Explain your answer.**

   _____

   _____

   _____

   _____

   _____

   _____

   _____

STOP

Name _____   Date _____

ELA4W2

Writing a Persuasive Essay

DIRECTIONS: Read the paragraph about a book one student really liked. Then answer each question below.

> I really liked the book *The Wizard of Oz* and think others will like it, too. It was very exciting, especially the part where Dorothy went to the Wicked Witch's castle and made the Witch melt. I also liked the way the characters worked together to solve their problems. Finally when Dorothy says, "There's no place like home," I thought about my home and the many wonderful things I have.

1. Think of a book you really liked. What is its title?

_____

_____

2. Why do you think others should read it?

_____

_____

_____

_____

_____

_____

3. What are some specific parts of the book that you think others would enjoy?

_____

_____

_____

_____

_____

_____

4. Now, think of an activity that you enjoy that you think others would enjoy as well. Explain why this activity is fun for you and the reasons your readers should try this activity. Be sure to use as many details as possible to persuade readers to try it.

_____

_____

_____

_____

_____

_____

_____

_____

_____

_____

_____

_____

_____

STOP

Using Organizational Features

DIRECTIONS: Study the table of contents and answer the questions that follow.

1. **Yoshi wants to find other resources that have information on sunken treasures. In which chapters should she look?**

   (A) chapters 1, 2, and 3
   (B) chapters 3, 4, and 5
   (C) chapters 4, 5, and 6
   (D) chapters 6, 7, and 8

2. **Which of the following sentences might be found in chapter 1?**

   (F) The Caribbean is a place many people think of when they hear the words *sunken treasure.*
   (G) One valuable site is *www.yo-ho-matey.com.*
   (H) Treasure ranges from ancient oil lamps to gold and jewels.
   (J) Many treasure ships sank during battles.

3. **Which chapter could help Yoshi identify sunken treasures that no one has claimed or recovered?**

   (A) chapter 2
   (B) chapter 3
   (C) chapter 4
   (D) chapter 5

4. **Yoshi wonders if there is an area that has more sunken treasure than any other area. Which chapter would be the most helpful?**

   (F) chapter 3
   (G) chapter 2
   (H) chapter 8
   (J) chapter 4

English/
Language Arts
Writing

ELA4W3

Using Reference Materials

DIRECTIONS: Use the picture of encyclopedias to answer questions 1–4.

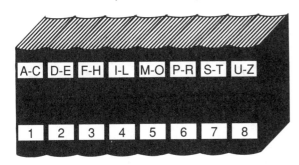

1. **In which volume would you find information about different types of flags?**

    (A) volume 2

    (B) volume 3

    (C) volume 5

    (D) volume 7

2. **Which of the following topics would be found in volume 5?**

    (F) information about the moon

    (G) how to knit

    (H) world climate regions

    (J) the life of Marian Anderson

3. **Where would you find an article about Thomas Jefferson?**

    (A) volume 7

    (B) volume 4

    (C) volume 1

    (D) volume 3

4. **Which of the following topics would be found in volume 1?**

    (F) bears

    (G) democracy

    (H) North America

    (J) Underground Railroad

5. **Look at these guide words from a dictionary page.**

    > **fourth–fragile**

    Which of the following could be found on this page?

    (A) frail

    (B) fourteenth

    (C) fracture

    (D) fountain

6. **Look at these guide words from a dictionary page.**

    > **pace–packing**

    Which of the following could be found on this page?

    (F) package

    (G) pac

    (H) pact

    (J) pad

7. **If a book's call number is 234.48, on which shelf would you find it?**

    (A) 800–890

    (B) 540–599

    (C) 220–285

    (D) 200–232

8. **Which of the following would you find on shelf 735–790?**

    (F) 700.989

    (G) 720.1

    (H) 748.88

    (J) 799.4

STOP

Editing and Revising

DIRECTIONS: Read the paragraphs and answer the questions that follow.

Volcanoes

(1) There are more than 15,000 active volcanoes in the world. **(2)** Still, know everything there is to know about volcanoes scientists do not. **(3)** The study of volcanoes is called volcanology, and people who study volcanoes are called volcanologists.

(4) How does a volcano form? **(5)** Hot liquid rock, called magma, bubbles toward the surface through rock. **(6)** Once magma has arrived at the earth's surface, it is called lava. **(7)** Lava builds up until it forms a mountain in the shape of a cone. **(8)** The spot where lava comes up to the earth's surface through the cone is called a volcano.

(9) Some volcanic eruptions calm, but others destructive. **(10)** Large pieces of rock can be thrown out of the volcano. **(11)** People near an erupting volcano can be in great danger from flowing lava and volcanic bombs.

---

1. **Sentence 2 is best written—**

   Ⓐ Scientists still don't know everything there is to know about volcanoes.

   Ⓑ Scientists don't know everything there is to know about volcanoes still.

   Ⓒ Scientists don't still know everything there is to know about volcanoes.

   Ⓓ as it is

2. **Which of these is not a sentence?**

   Ⓕ sentence 8
   Ⓖ sentence 9
   Ⓗ sentence 10
   Ⓙ sentence 11

3. **Which sentence could be added after sentence 10?**

   Ⓐ Some people collect these rocks after the eruption.

   Ⓑ Dust is also thrown out and can cloud the air.

   Ⓒ Rocks are also formed.

   Ⓓ Sometimes the rocks come out with so much force they are called volcanic bombs.

4. **In sentence 11, *flowing* is best written—**

   Ⓕ flowdering
   Ⓖ flowering
   Ⓗ flowed
   Ⓙ as it is

English/
Language Arts

Spelling

ELA4W4

DIRECTIONS: Find the word that is spelled correctly and fits best in the blank.

1. **Please _____ your work.**

   (A) revew

   (B) reeview

   (C) review

   (D) raview

2. **He is my best _____ .**

   (F) frind

   (G) frend

   (H) friend

   (J) freind

3. **We can _____ the gymnasium.**

   (A) decarate

   (B) decorait

   (C) decorrate

   (D) decorate

4. **The store is in a good _____ .**

   (F) locashun

   (G) locashin

   (H) locatin

   (J) location

5. **Students were _____ for bravery.**

   (A) honored

   (B) honord

   (C) honered

   (D) honard

6. **The train _____ arrived.**

   (F) finaly

   (G) finnalie

   (H) finely

   (J) finally

DIRECTIONS: Read each answer. Choose the answer that has a spelling error. If there are no errors, choose "no mistakes."

7. (A) service

    (B) fountain

    (C) suceed

    (D) no mistakes

8. (F) recieve

    (G) observe

    (H) information

    (J) no mistakes

9. (A) jury

    (B) knuckle

    (C) pollite

    (D) no mistakes

10. (F) wildernes

    (G) structure

    (H) republic

    (J) no mistakes

STOP

English/
Language Arts

ELA4W4

Punctuation

DIRECTIONS: Read each sentence. Choose the punctuation mark that is needed in the sentence. If no more punctuation is needed, choose "none."

1. **Do you think the film is scary**
   - (A) .
   - (B) !
   - (C) ?
   - (D) none

2. **Jody please don't forget to feed the cat.**
   - (F) ?
   - (G) !
   - (H) ,
   - (J) none

3. **Sharla Kristin, and Kylie all went to the movies.**
   - (A) .
   - (B) !
   - (C) ,
   - (D) none

4. **The clouds were dark, and the wind was getting stronger.**
   - (F) !
   - (G) .
   - (H) ?
   - (J) none

5. **"Should I bring an umbrella" asked Martha.**
   - (A) ,
   - (B) ?
   - (C) !
   - (D) none

6. **Mrs Hines brought the cherry pie to the bake sale.**
   - (F) .
   - (G) !
   - (H) ,
   - (J) none

7. **Yes I would like to join the team.**
   - (A) ?
   - (B) .
   - (C) ,
   - (D) none

8. **Look out**
   - (F) ,
   - (G) .
   - (H) !
   - (J) none

9. **Did you know theyre going sledding today?**
   - (A) .
   - (B) ,
   - (C) !
   - (D) none

10. **My favorite sport is soccer.**
    - (F) ,
    - (G) .
    - (H) !
    - (J) none

STOP

44

English/
Language Arts

Mini-Test 3

ELA4W1–ELA4W4

For pages 35–44

DIRECTIONS: Choose the best answer.

1. **Which of the following types of writing would be a response to literature?**
   - (A) a letter to a friend
   - (B) a research report
   - (C) a book review
   - (D) a short story

2. **Which of the following types of writing would *not* be a persuasive essay?**
   - (F) a review of your favorite book that describes why others should read it
   - (G) a letter to the editor explaining why your community should have a new park
   - (H) a story about your family's vacation
   - (J) a letter to your parents stating the reasons you should get an increase in your allowance

3. **If you were writing a report about the different types of hawks, your report would be _____ .**
   - (A) a response to literature
   - (B) a narrative piece
   - (C) informational writing
   - (D) an entertaining story

4. **Which of the following does not have to be included in a narrative?**
   - (F) descriptions of the characters
   - (G) steps that are easy to follow
   - (H) a description of the setting
   - (J) a plot

5. **What is the name of the part of a book in which references are listed?**
   - (A) bibliography
   - (B) table of contents
   - (C) index
   - (D) glossary

6. **Which word would be a heading for the other words in an outline?**
   - (F) Cans
   - (G) Recycling
   - (H) Glass
   - (J) Paper

7. **Which punctuation mark is needed in this sentence?**

   Oranges lemons, and grapefruits are citrus fruits.
   - (A) ?
   - (B) ,
   - (C) !
   - (D) .

8. **Which answer has a spelling error?**
   - (F) reproduce
   - (G) usualy
   - (H) interest
   - (J) journal

STOP

Conventions Standards

Conventions are essential for reading, writing, and speaking. Instruction in language conventions will, therefore, occur within the context of reading, writing, and speaking, rather than in isolation. The student writes to make connections with the larger world. A student's ideas are more likely to be taken seriously when the words are spelled accurately and the sentences are grammatically correct. Use of Standard English conventions helps readers understand and follow the student's meaning, while errors can be distracting and confusing. Standard English conventions are the "good manners" of writing and speaking that make communication fluid.

ELA4C1. The student demonstrates understanding and control of the rules of the English language, realizing that usage involves the appropriate application of conventions and grammar in both written and spoken formats. *(See pages 47–54.)* The student:

a. recognizes the subject-predicate relationship in sentences.
b. uses and identifies four basic parts of speech (adjective, noun, verb, adverb).
c. uses and identifies correct mechanics (end marks, commas for series, capitalization), correct usage (subject and verb agreement in a simple sentence), and correct sentence structure (elimination of sentence fragments).
d. uses and identifies words or word parts from other languages that have been adopted into the English language.
e. writes legibly in cursive, leaving space between letters in a word and between words in a sentence.
f. uses knowledge of letter sounds, word parts, word segmentation, and syllabication to monitor and correct spelling.
g. spells most commonly used homophones correctly (there, they're, their; two, too, to).
h. varies the sentence structure by kind (declarative, interrogative, imperative, and exclamatory sentences and functional fragments), order, and complexity (simple, compound).

Conventions

Nouns and Pronouns

DIRECTIONS: Choose the pronoun that completes the sentence best.

1. **Chang and Audrey made _____ kites together.**
   - (A) him
   - (B) she
   - (C) them
   - (D) their

2. **Are _____ parents coming to the concert?**
   - (F) she
   - (G) he
   - (H) her
   - (J) it

3. **_____ spoke to my mother on Parents' Night.**
   - (A) Him
   - (B) He
   - (C) Us
   - (D) Them

DIRECTIONS: Choose the answer that could replace the underlined word or words.

4. **<u>Jill and Keisha</u> went to soccer practice.**
   - (F) Him
   - (G) Them
   - (H) They
   - (J) She

5. **Did <u>Brian</u> find his lost cat?**
   - (A) him
   - (B) he
   - (C) it
   - (D) us

DIRECTIONS: Write a proper noun for each common noun. Write a common noun for each proper noun.

6. country _____

7. boy _____

8. lake _____

9. California _____

DIRECTIONS: Draw a line under each noun. Circle each pronoun.

10. **Yolanda walked her sister to school.**

11. **Karen and I played volleyball with our friends.**

12. **My father and Uncle Ken attended their club meeting.**

13. **Toby made a new dress.**

14. **Randy and Father are planting corn seeds.**

STOP

Adjectives and Adverbs

 An adjective is a word that describes a noun or pronoun.

DIRECTIONS: Circle the adjective(s) in each sentence.

1. Danielle picked red and yellow roses from her garden.

2. Those pupils passed their spelling test.

3. This man is our new teacher.

4. Both children attended the birthday party.

5. My parents are busy people.

6. Spot is a playful, frisky dog.

7. Please sharpen these pencils, Frank.

8. Rudy hit two home runs in that game.

9. Judy bought two peaches and one red apple.

10. My kite glided through the bright blue sky.

11. Ira moved to the smallest town in Montana.

12. There are twelve boys and fourteen girls in Kit's class.

13. Devon read his book under the shady elm tree.

 An adverb is a word that describes a verb, adjective, or another adverb. It usually tells when, how, where, or how often something is done and ends in *-ly*.

DIRECTIONS: Circle the adverb in each sentence.

14. Jerry behaved badly.

15. The rain fell gently.

16. I will surely pass the test.

17. The children sang happily.

18. The stream rushed by swiftly.

19. Jill came by early.

20. The stars glittered brightly.

21. The neighbors' dog barked loudly.

22. Mr. Ito drove carefully.

**English/
Language Arts**

ELA4C1

Verbs

Conventions

 Clue If you aren't sure which answer is correct, read each choice quietly to yourself.

DIRECTIONS: Choose the answer that best completes the sentence.

1. **Jeff and Channa _____ us make bread.**
   - (A) had help
   - (B) will help
   - (C) helps
   - (D) helping

2. **Please _____ this letter to the post office.**
   - (F) took
   - (G) has taken
   - (H) tooked
   - (J) take

3. **No one _____ him about the change of plans.**
   - (A) telled
   - (B) told
   - (C) tells
   - (D) did tell

4. **The gift _____ yesterday.**
   - (F) arrives
   - (G) arrived
   - (H) arriving
   - (J) will arrive

DIRECTIONS: Choose the answer that uses an incorrect verb.

5.
   - (A) The library have a room for music.
   - (B) In the room, you can listen to tapes.
   - (C) The room has lots of books about music.
   - (D) I love spending time there.

6.
   - (F) Chang has pick up her heavy backpack.
   - (G) She carries that backpack everywhere.
   - (H) It has all her art supplies in it.
   - (J) She also carries her laptop in the backpack.

7.
   - (A) He forgot to take his jacket home.
   - (B) It were a cold day.
   - (C) He shivered without his jacket.
   - (D) He was very glad to get home at last.

8.
   - (F) Nobody is home today.
   - (G) The house is locked up.
   - (H) It look strange with the shades down.
   - (J) I am not used to seeing it so empty.

STOP

**English/
Language Arts**

ELA4C1

Capitalization
and Punctuation

DIRECTIONS: Rewrite the sentences below using the correct capitalization and punctuation.

1. **Tyson began singing the star-spangled banner**

   _____

   _____

   _____

   _____

2. **Joe read an article about canadian geese in a magazine called migrating birds**

   _____

   _____

   _____

   _____

3. **We sold school supplies to help raise money for the red cross.**

   _____

   _____

   _____

   _____

4. **I'm really glad you are here Abby said**

   _____

   _____

   _____

   _____

DIRECTIONS: Choose the sentence that shows correct punctuation and capitalization.

5.
   (A) Tell Mrs Jensen I called.
   (B) Miss. Richards will be late.
   (C) Our coach is Mr. Wannamaker
   (D) Dr. Cullinane was here earlier.

6.
   (F) Will you please take the garbage out
   (G) Dont let Rachel forget her chores.
   (H) She has been reading *Charlotte's Web* all afternoon.
   (J) This house looks like a pigsty

7.
   (A) "I suggest you go the library to do research," Mom said.
   (B) "The *world book encyclopedia* is a good place to look."
   (C) "I will help you look in *National Geographic* when you get home.
   (D) Your report will be perfect when you're done," Mom insisted.

8.
   (F) Joel hurt his wrist, yesterday while playing hockey.
   (G) However, he scored three goals in the process.
   (H) He will be the champion of patterson Ice Center.
   (J) Perhaps they will loan him the stanley cup

STOP

**English/
Language Arts**

Conventions

Greek and Latin Roots

ELA4C1

DIRECTIONS: Read each question. Choose the English word that comes from the Latin or Greek word defined in the question.

1. **Which of these words probably comes from the Greek word *mikros,* meaning small?**
   - (A) microscope
   - (B) meter
   - (C) macaroni
   - (D) motor

2. **Which of these words probably comes from the Latin word *centum,* meaning hundred?**
   - (F) recent
   - (G) ocean
   - (H) century
   - (J) sent

3. **Which of these words probably comes from the Latin word *circuitus,* meaning going around?**
   - (A) curious
   - (B) circuit
   - (C) cirrus
   - (D) cut

4. **Which of these words probably comes from the Greek word *bios,* meaning life?**
   - (F) biology
   - (G) bicycle
   - (H) bison
   - (J) binocular

5. **Which of these words probably comes from the Latin word *lampein,* meaning to shine?**
   - (A) lampoon
   - (B) lament
   - (C) lamp
   - (D) lamprey

6. **Which of these words probably comes from the Latin word *magnus,* meaning great?**
   - (F) magnet
   - (G) mangle
   - (H) major
   - (J) minor

7. **Which of these words probably comes from the Latin word *bene,* meaning good?**
   - (A) beneath
   - (B) bendable
   - (C) bentwood
   - (D) benefit

8. **Which of these words probably comes from the Latin word *tactus,* meaning touch?**
   - (F) tactic
   - (G) contact
   - (H) taco
   - (J) retract

STOP

**English/
Language Arts**

ELA4C1

Dividing Words
into Syllables

DIRECTIONS: Rewrite the following words divided into syllables.

Below are some of the rules for dividing words into syllables:

1. **Closed:** These syllables end in a consonant. The vowel sound is generally short. (Examples: *rab/bit, nap/kin*)

2. **Open:** These syllables end in a vowel. The vowel sound is usually long. (Examples: *ti/ger, pi/lot*)

3. **Vowel-silent e:** These generally represent long-vowel sounds. (Examples: *com/pete, de/cide*)

4. **Consonant -le:** Usually when -*le* appears at the end of a word and a consonant comes before it, the consonant plus -*le* make up the last syllable. (Examples: *ta/ble, sta/ble*)

1. potato

_____

2. provide

_____

3. circus

_____

4. clothing

_____

5. couple

_____

6. decorate

_____

7. destroy

_____

8. double

_____

9. finger

_____

10. happen

_____

11. height

_____

12. ledge

_____

English/
Language Arts

ELA4C1

Identifying Types of Sentences

DIRECTIONS: Below are several sentences. Identify what type of sentence each one is by writing **DE** for declarative, **IN** for interrogative, **IM** for imperative, and **EX** for exclamatory.

Examples:

A **declarative** sentence makes a statement and has a period at the end.
Ben walked home from school with Jaime.

An **interrogative** sentence asks a question and ends with a question mark.
Will you feed the fish today?

And **exclamatory** sentence shows excitement or emotion and ends with an exclamation mark.
Hey! Stop hitting me!

An **imperative** sentence expresses a command or request and ends with a period.
Come to the principal's office now.

_____ 1. He quickly looked around to see if anyone was watching him.

_____ 2. He fled toward the barn.

_____ 3. Can you keep a secret?

_____ 4. Not a chance!

_____ 5. Do not stop reading until you reach the end of this story.

_____ 6. Jack stood on the deck of the ship.

_____ 7. Get back in your room.

_____ 8. What kind of cat do you have?

_____ 9. What a joke!

_____ 10. They looked for a place to hide their treasure.

_____ 11. Where do you want to eat lunch?

_____ 12. Don't touch that picture.

_____ 13. I think I forgot my lunch at home.

_____ 14. Mom is going to be mad at me!

_____ 15. What are you going to do?

STOP

Name _____ Date _____

Varying Sentence Structure

DIRECTIONS: Write **S** before each line that is a simple sentence. Write **F** before each line that is a sentence fragment.

1. _____ **You should know better.**

2. _____ **Walking faster all the time.**

3. _____ **Wait outside.**

4. _____ **Caught the ball and threw it to second base.**

5. _____ **Every house in town.**

6. _____ **The dog jumped over the fence.**

7. _____ **They will arrive soon.**

8. _____ **Can you close the window?**

9. _____ **A few people in this club.**

10. _____ **He can read well.**

DIRECTIONS: Choose the answer that best combines the underlined sentences.

11. **Pedro finished his homework.**
    Pedro went to bed.

    (A) Pedro finished his homework or went to bed.

    (B) Pedro finished his homework and then went to bed.

    (C) Pedro finished his homework because he went to bed.

    (D) Going to bed, Pedro finished his homework

12. **The truck brought the furniture to our house. The truck was large.**

    (F) The large truck, which brought the furniture to our house.

    (G) The truck was large that brought the furniture to our house.

    (H) The truck brought the furniture to our house, and was large.

    (J) The large truck brought the furniture to our house.

DIRECTIONS: A *compound sentence* is made up of two complete thoughts, or simple sentences, that are joined by a conjunction. Use the conjunctions *and, or,* or *but* after the comma to complete each sentence.

13. **Sasha flew to Chicago, _____ she took a train to Milwaukee.**

14. **I can go to the game, _____ I have to be home by ten.**

15. **Finish your homework, _____ you won't be allowed to play outside.**

16. **Some athletes are paid well, _____ others do not make much money.**

17. **His favorite food is pizza, _____ his favorite drink is lemonade.**

18. **Miss Steiner is known as a poet, _____ she can also sing and dance.**

19. **You can spend your money on ice cream, _____ you can save your money to buy a toy.**

STOP

54

English/
Language Arts

ELA4C1

For pages 47–54

Mini-Test 4

DIRECTIONS: Choose the best answer.

1. **Which pronoun could replace the underlined words in this sentence?**

   I have not seen <u>your parents</u> this weekend.

   (A) they

   (B) them

   (C) their

   (D) us

2. **In which of the following sentences is the adjective underlined?**

   (F) She <u>picked</u> a yellow daisy.

   (G) They went to the <u>gym</u>.

   (H) The cat curled up on the <u>soft</u> blanket.

   (J) I love to <u>eat</u> pizza.

3. **In which of the following sentences is the adverb underlined?**

   (A) He ate a <u>sour</u> grape.

   (B) He ran <u>quickly</u> to catch up with the others.

   (C) Both <u>puppies</u> are black and white.

   (D) She <u>chewed</u> her gum loudly.

4. **In which of the following sentences is the verb underlined?**

   (F) She <u>licked</u> her ice cream cone.

   (G) I bought a new <u>bike</u>.

   (H) The kite flew <u>high</u> in the sky.

   (J) I broke a <u>dish</u> in the kitchen.

5. **Which of these words probably comes from the French word *ravager,* meaning to uproot?**

   (A) ravage

   (B) ravel

   (C) rave

   (D) ravine

6. **Which word is correctly divided into syllables?**

   (F) rabb/it

   (G) ti/ger

   (H) compl/ete

   (J) tab/le

DIRECTIONS: Choose the answer that shows correct punctuation and capitalization.

7. (A) The house is very large

   (B) what did you say?

   (C) The Tennis courts are full.

   (D) Kaylie put our names on the list.

8. (F) Tell Mrs Jensen I called.

   (G) Miss. Richards will be late.

   (H) Our coach is Mr. Slate.

   (J) Did you remember your homework assignment

DIRECTIONS: Choose the answer that best combines the underlined sentences.

9. <u>**Arnie found a ball.**</u>
   <u>**The ball was red.**</u>
   <u>**He found it on the way to school.**</u>

   (A) Finding a red ball, Arnie was on his way to school.

   (B) Arnie found a red ball on the way to school.

   (C) Arnie found a ball on the way to school that was red.

   (D) The red ball that Arnie found on the way to school.

Listening, Speaking, and Viewing Standards

The student demonstrates an understanding of listening, speaking, and viewing skills for a variety of purposes. The student listens critically and responds appropriately to oral communication in a variety of genres and media. The student speaks in a manner that guides the listener to understand important ideas.

ELA4LSV1. The student participates in student-to-teacher, student-to-student, and group verbal interactions. The student:
a. initiates new topics in addition to responding to adult-initiated topics.
b. asks relevant questions.
c. responds to questions with appropriate information.
d. uses language cues to indicate different levels of certainty or hypothesizing (e.g., "What if. . ."; "Very likely. . ."; "I'm unsure whether. . .").
e. confirms understanding by paraphrasing the adult's directions or suggestions.
f. displays appropriate turn-taking behaviors.
g. actively solicits another person's comments or opinions.
h. offers own opinion assertively without domineering.
i. responds appropriately to comments and questions.
j. volunteers contributions and responds when directly solicited by teacher or discussion leader.
k. gives reasons in support of opinions expressed.
l. clarifies, illustrates, or expands on a response when asked to do so; asks classmates for similar expansions.

ELA4LSV2. The student listens to and views various forms of text and media in order to gather and share information, persuade others, and express and understand ideas.
When responding to <u>visual and oral texts and media</u> (e.g., television, radio, film productions, and electronic media), the student:
a. demonstrates an awareness of the presence of the media in the daily lives of most people.
b. evaluates the role of the media in focusing attention and in forming an opinion.
c. judges the extent to which the media provides a source of entertainment as well as a source of information.

When delivering or responding to <u>presentations</u>, the student:
a. shapes information to achieve a particular purpose and to appeal to the interests and background knowledge of audience members.
b. uses notes, multimedia, or other memory aids to structure the presentation.
c. engages the audience with appropriate verbal cues and eye contact.
d. projects a sense of individuality and personality in selecting and organizing content and in delivery.
e. shapes content and organization according to criteria for importance and impact rather than according to availability of information in resource materials.

How Am I Doing?

Mini-Test 1

Pages 21–22

Number Correct

10 answers correct	**Great Job!** Move on to the section test on page 59.
7–9 answers correct	**You're almost there!** But you still need a little practice. Review practice pages 8–20 before moving on to the section test on page 59.
0–6 answers correct	**Oops!** Time to review what you have learned and try again. Review the practice section on pages 8–20. Then retake the test on pages 21–22. Now move on to the section test on page 59.

Mini-Test 2

Page 32

Number Correct

7 answers correct	**Awesome!** Move on to the section test on page 59.
4–6 answers correct	**You're almost there!** But you still need a little practice. Review practice pages 25–31 before moving on to the section test on page 59.
0–3 answers correct	**Oops!** Time to review what you have learned and try again. Review the practice section on pages 25–31. Then retake the test on page 32. Now move on to the section test on page 59.

Mini-Test 3

Page 45

Number Correct

8 answers correct	**Great Job!** Move on to the section test on page 59.
4–7 answers correct	**You're almost there!** But you still need a little practice. Review practice pages 35–43 before moving on to the section test on page 59.
0–3 answers correct	**Oops!** Time to review what you have learned and try again. Review the practice section on pages 35–43. Then retake the test on page 45. Now move on to the section test on page 59.

How Am I Doing?

Mini-Test 4	9 answers correct	**Awesome!** Move on to the section test on page 59.
Page 55 **Number Correct**	5–8 answers correct	**You're almost there!** But you still need a little practice. Review practice pages 47–54 before moving on to the section test on page 59.
	0–4 answers correct	**Oops!** Time to review what you have learned and try again. Review the practice section on pages 47–54. Then retake the test on page 55. Now move on to the section test on page 59.

Name _____   Date _____

Final English/Language Arts Test
for pages 8–55

DIRECTIONS: Read the passage, and then answer the questions.

Home Alone

"Are you sure you're going to be all right at home alone?" Yong's mother asked.

"Yes, Mom," Yong replied, trying not to roll her eyes. "I'm old enough to stay here alone for three hours." Yong's mom and dad were going to a barbecue that afternoon. Since kids weren't invited, Yong was staying home alone. It was the first time her parents had left her home by herself. Yong was a little nervous, but she was sure she could handle it.

"Let me give you a last-minute quiz to make sure," her dad said. Yong's father was a teacher, and he was always giving her little tests. "What happens if somebody calls and asks for your mom or me?"

"I tell them that you are busy and can't come to the phone right now," Yong said. "Then I take a message."

"What if there is a knock on the door?" asked her dad.

"I don't answer it, because I can't let anyone in anyway."

"Okay, here's a tough one." Her father looked very serious. "What if you hear ghosts in the closets?"

"Dad!" Yong giggled. "Our house isn't haunted. I'll be fine. Look, I have the phone number of the house where you'll be, so I can call if I need to. I've got the numbers for the police, the fire department, and the poison control center. I won't turn on the stove or leave the house. And, I'll double lock the doors behind you when you leave."

Yong's parents were satisfied. They hugged her good-bye and left for the afternoon. Yong sat for a few minutes and enjoyed the quiet of the empty house. Then she went to the kitchen to fix herself a snack. She opened the cupboard door. Then she jumped back, startled. There was a ghost in the cupboard! Yong laughed and laughed. Her dad had taped up a picture of a ghost. It said, "BOO! We love you!"

1. What is the setting of this story?

- (A) the beach
- (B) a barbecue
- (C) Yong's house
- (D) a haunted house

2. What is the plot of this story?

- (F) Yong's dad does not trust her.
- (G) Yong is staying home by herself for the first time.
- (H) Yong finds a ghost in the cupboard.
- (J) Yong does not want to stay home alone.

3. What is the main reason Yong's dad keeps asking her questions?

- (A) He wants to make sure she knows all the emergency phone numbers.
- (B) He wants to make sure she will be safe while they are gone.
- (C) He likes giving her quizzes.
- (D) He played a trick on her.

4. Who are the main characters in this story?

- (F) Yong, her mom, and her dad
- (G) Yong and her friend Sam
- (H) Yong, her dad, and the dog
- (J) Yong and her dad

5. What do you learn about Yong's dad?

- (A) He has a good job.
- (B) He is very serious.
- (C) He is very quiet.
- (D) He has a good sense of humor.

GO

Name _____   Date _____

DIRECTIONS: Read the passage, and then answer the questions.

Helping the Mountain Gorilla

Mountain gorillas live in the rain forests in Rwanda, Uganda, and the Democratic Republic of the Congo. These large, beautiful animals are becoming very rare. They have lost much of their habitat as people move in and take over gorillas' lands. Although there are strict laws protecting gorillas, poachers continue to hunt them.

Scientists observe gorillas to learn about their habits and needs. Then scientists write about their findings in magazines. Concerned readers sometimes contribute money to help safeguard the mountain gorillas.

Many other people are working hard to protect the mountain gorillas. Park rangers patrol the rain forest and arrest poachers. Tourists bring much-needed money into the area, encouraging local residents to protect the gorillas, too.

6. **What is this passage mainly about?**
   - (F) mountain gorillas' family relationships
   - (G) scientists who study mountain gorillas
   - (H) ways that gorillas are threatened and helped
   - (J) poachers and wars that threaten gorillas' survival

7. **Which words help you figure out the meaning of *habitat*?**
   - (A) "large, beautiful animals"
   - (B) "gorillas' lands"
   - (C) "the human population"
   - (D) "recent civil wars"

8. **The author's purpose for writing this passage is _____ .**
   - (F) to entertain readers
   - (G) to inform readers about mountain gorillas
   - (H) to motivate readers to visit Rwanda
   - (J) to explain to readers where Africa is

9. **Which of the following is a fact?**
   - (A) Mountain gorillas are beautiful animals.
   - (B) Mountain gorillas live in the rain forests in Rwanda, Uganda, and the Democratic Republic of the Congo.
   - (C) Everyone should send money to help the gorillas.
   - (D) Scientists work to arrest poachers.

DIRECTIONS: Choose the meaning for each underlined word.

10. **We were <u>exhausted</u> after running. Exhausted means _____ .**
    - (F) very tired
    - (G) refreshed
    - (H) excited
    - (J) wide awake

11. **I <u>sprinted</u> to the finish line. Sprinted means _____ .**
    - (A) skipped
    - (B) crawled
    - (C) ran very quickly
    - (D) tripped

DIRECTIONS: Choose the word that correctly completes both sentences.

12. **Someone bought the _____ on the corner.**
    A new house costs a _____ of money.
    - (F) bunch
    - (G) lot
    - (H) house
    - (J) property

GO

Name _____   Date _____

13. Inez bought a _____ of soda.

    The doctor said it was a difficult _____ .

    (A) case

    (B) carton

    (C) disease

    (D) situation

DIRECTIONS: Choose the best answer.

14. **What prefix can you add to the root word**
satisfied **to make a word that means**
"not satisfied."

    (F) re-

    (G) anti-

    (H) dis-

    (J) pre-

DIRECTIONS: Choose the word that means the same
or about the same as the underlined word.

15. <u>high</u> fence

    (A) tall

    (B) happy

    (C) long

    (D) wide

16. <u>paste</u> the paper

    (F) fold

    (G) attach

    (H) patch

    (J) glue

17. <u>chilly</u> day

    (A) long

    (B) frozen

    (C) cold

    (D) unpleasant

DIRECTIONS: Choose the word that means the
opposite of the underlined word.

18. <u>valuable</u> painting

    (F) strange

    (G) expensive

    (H) worthless

    (J) humorous

19. <u>loose</u> tie

    (A) tight

    (B) lost

    (C) plain

    (D) ill fitting

DIRECTIONS: Choose the best answer.

20. **Ahmed is writing a report on the whales that**
live in the Indian Ocean. Where should he look
for general information about whales?

    (F) an atlas

    (G) an almanac

    (H) an encyclopedia

    (J) a newspaper

21. **Which of these is the best resource for maps**
of the Indian Ocean?

    (A) an atlas

    (B) an almanac

    (C) an encyclopedia

    (D) a newspaper

22. **Look at these guide words from a dictionary**
page.

> **nothing–now**

    Which of the following could be found on this
page?

    (F) novel

    (G) nose

    (H) notepaper

    (J) nowhere

GO

23. If a book's call number is 653.12, on which shelf would you find it at the library?

- (A) 500–600
- (B) 600–700
- (C) 700–800
- (D) 800–900

24. In an outline, which of these words would be the best heading for the other words?

- (F) People
- (G) Government
- (H) Climate
- (J) Bolivia

DIRECTIONS: Use the picture of encyclopedias to answer the questions.

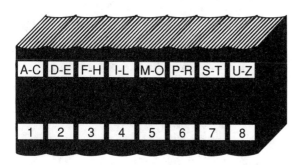

25. Which of the following topics would be found in volume 7?

- (A) information about the solar system
- (B) how magnets work
- (C) the habitat of pandas
- (D) a map of Russia

26. In which volume would you find information about different types of lizards?

- (F) volume 2
- (G) volume 4
- (H) volume 5
- (J) volume 7

DIRECTIONS: Greg is writing a story for the Young Author's column of the school paper.

The first draft of the story needs some editing. Here is the first part of the story.

(1) Our town's name is Lost City. **(2)** It has an unusual history. **(3)** First of all, it was founded in 1886 by accident. **(4)** A group of pioneers thought they were headed toward San Francisco. **(5)** Instead, they ended up hundreds of miles farther up the coast.

27. Which of these best combines sentences 1 and 2 into one sentence?

- (A) Lost City has an unusual history and it is our town.
- (B) An unusual history, our town is Lost City.
- (C) Our town, Lost City, has an unusual history.
- (D) With an unusual history, our town is Lost City.

28. Which is the best way to write sentence 4?

- (F) A group of pioneers toward San Francisco were headed.
- (G) Toward San Francisco a group of pioneers thought they were headed.
- (H) San Francisco, they thought the pioneers were headed.
- (J) as it is

Now read the next part of the story.

(1) The founders of Lost City from Baltimore came. **(2)** They knew about fishing, trapping crabs, and gathering oysters and clams. **(3)** It was only natural that they would use their skills in the Pacific Ocean. **(4)** Soon, Lost City was known for its fine seafood. **(5)** Wagons packed with ice and snow brought fish, oysters, and crabs to inland towns. **(6)** Seafood restaurants were on almost every corner.

29. Select the best way to write sentence 1.

- (A) The founders of Lost City came from Baltimore.
- (B) From Baltimore the founders of Lost City came.
- (C) Coming from Baltimore were the founders of Lost City.
- (D) as it is

DIRECTIONS: Choose the answer that best completes the sentence.

30. Is _____ going to the park with us?

- (F) she
- (G) them
- (H) her
- (J) it

31. Yesterday, Kara _____ us about her trip to Scotland.

- (A) telled
- (B) told
- (C) tells
- (D) did told

32. He _____ the windows carefully.

- (F) wipe
- (G) did wiping
- (H) wiping
- (J) wiped

33. Please give me the _____ doll on the shelf.

- (A) largest
- (B) more large
- (C) most large
- (D) larger

34. The team clapped _____ when he scored a goal.

- (F) loudest
- (G) most loud
- (H) loud
- (J) loudly

DIRECTIONS: Choose the line that has a punctuation error. If there is no error, choose "no mistakes."

35.
- (A) The bus will pick us up
- (B) at 830 a.m. sharp for
- (C) the field trip to the zoo.
- (D) no mistakes

36.
- (F) Sara wanted to adopt
- (G) another greyhound but
- (H) she simply didn't have room.
- (J) no mistakes

37.
- (A) Clare, Andrea and I
- (B) were next in line
- (C) for the roller coaster.
- (D) no mistakes

DIRECTIONS: Choose the answer that fits best in the blank and shows correct capitalization and punctuation.

38. The new mall will open on _____ .

- (F) may 1 2004
- (G) May 1, 2004
- (H) may 1, 2004
- (J) May, 1, 2004

39. Do you think we should go swimming, _____

- (A) Sam?
- (B) sam.
- (C) sam!
- (D) Sam.

GO

Name _____ Date _____

DIRECTIONS: Read each answer. Choose the answer that has a spelling error. If there are no errors, choose "no mistakes."

40. 　(F)　recieve
　　(G)　observe
　　(H)　information
　　(J)　no mistakes

41. 　(A)　jury
　　(B)　knuckle
　　(C)　pollite
　　(D)　no mistakes

42. 　(F)　wildernes
　　(G)　structure
　　(H)　republic
　　(J)　no mistakes

DIRECTIONS: Choose the best answer.

43. **Which of the following words in correctly divided into syllables?**
　　(A)　ess/ay
　　(B)　capt/ain
　　(C)　per/fect
　　(D)　troub/le

44. **Which of the following sentences is an example of a declarative sentence?**
　　(F)　What did you get for your birthday?
　　(G)　I can't believe it!
　　(H)　It was a very cold day.
　　(J)　Bring me the book that is on the counter.

45. **Which of the following sentences is an example of an interrogative sentence?**
　　(A)　You've got to be kidding!
　　(B)　What time is it?
　　(C)　Don't run out in the street.
　　(D)　Darcy went to the store.

46. **Which of the following sentences is a fragment?**
　　(F)　Her favorite color is blue.
　　(G)　She wears it every day.
　　(H)　While she sometimes wears pink.
　　(J)　She never wears the color green.

47. **Which conjunction would fit best in the blank?**

Turner studies hard for his tests, _____ he gets good grades.
　　(A)　but
　　(B)　and
　　(C)　for
　　(D)　or

DIRECTIONS: Choose the answer that best combines the underlined sentences.

48. **The room was filled with children. The children were happy.**
　　(F)　The room was filled with happy children.
　　(G)　The room was filled and the children were happy.
　　(H)　The children were happy who filled the room.
　　(J)　Filled with happy children was the room.

Name _____   Date _____

Final English/Language Arts Test
Answer Sheet

1	Ⓐ Ⓑ Ⓒ Ⓓ	31	Ⓐ Ⓑ Ⓒ Ⓓ
2	Ⓕ Ⓖ Ⓗ Ⓙ	32	Ⓕ Ⓖ Ⓗ Ⓙ
3	Ⓐ Ⓑ Ⓒ Ⓓ	33	Ⓐ Ⓑ Ⓒ Ⓓ
4	Ⓕ Ⓖ Ⓗ Ⓙ	34	Ⓕ Ⓖ Ⓗ Ⓙ
5	Ⓐ Ⓑ Ⓒ Ⓓ	35	Ⓐ Ⓑ Ⓒ Ⓓ
6	Ⓕ Ⓖ Ⓗ Ⓙ	36	Ⓕ Ⓖ Ⓗ Ⓙ
7	Ⓐ Ⓑ Ⓒ Ⓓ	37	Ⓐ Ⓑ Ⓒ Ⓓ
8	Ⓕ Ⓖ Ⓗ Ⓙ	38	Ⓕ Ⓖ Ⓗ Ⓙ
9	Ⓐ Ⓑ Ⓒ Ⓓ	39	Ⓐ Ⓑ Ⓒ Ⓓ
10	Ⓕ Ⓖ Ⓗ Ⓙ	40	Ⓕ Ⓖ Ⓗ Ⓙ
11	Ⓐ Ⓑ Ⓒ Ⓓ	41	Ⓐ Ⓑ Ⓒ Ⓓ
12	Ⓕ Ⓖ Ⓗ Ⓙ	42	Ⓕ Ⓖ Ⓗ Ⓙ
13	Ⓐ Ⓑ Ⓒ Ⓓ	43	Ⓐ Ⓑ Ⓒ Ⓓ
14	Ⓕ Ⓖ Ⓗ Ⓙ	44	Ⓕ Ⓖ Ⓗ Ⓙ
15	Ⓐ Ⓑ Ⓒ Ⓓ	45	Ⓐ Ⓑ Ⓒ Ⓓ
16	Ⓕ Ⓖ Ⓗ Ⓙ	46	Ⓕ Ⓖ Ⓗ Ⓙ
17	Ⓐ Ⓑ Ⓒ Ⓓ	47	Ⓐ Ⓑ Ⓒ Ⓓ
18	Ⓕ Ⓖ Ⓗ Ⓙ	48	Ⓕ Ⓖ Ⓗ Ⓙ
19	Ⓐ Ⓑ Ⓒ Ⓓ		
20	Ⓕ Ⓖ Ⓗ Ⓙ		
21	Ⓐ Ⓑ Ⓒ Ⓓ		
22	Ⓕ Ⓖ Ⓗ Ⓙ		
23	Ⓐ Ⓑ Ⓒ Ⓓ		
24	Ⓕ Ⓖ Ⓗ Ⓙ		
25	Ⓐ Ⓑ Ⓒ Ⓓ		
26	Ⓕ Ⓖ Ⓗ Ⓙ		
27	Ⓐ Ⓑ Ⓒ Ⓓ		
28	Ⓕ Ⓖ Ⓗ Ⓙ		
29	Ⓐ Ⓑ Ⓒ Ⓓ		
30	Ⓕ Ⓖ Ⓗ Ⓙ		

Georgia Mathematics
Content Standards

The mathematics section measures knowledge in six different areas:

* 1) **Number and Operations**

2) **Measurement**

3) **Geometry**

4) **Algebra**

5) **Data Analysis**

6) **Process Skills**

Georgia Mathematics
Table of Contents

Number and Operations Standards

M4N. Number and Operations

Students will further develop their understanding of whole numbers and master the four basic operations with whole numbers by solving problems. They will also understand rounding and when to appropriately use it. Students will add and subtract decimal fractions and common fractions with common denominators.

M4N1. Students will further develop their understanding of how whole numbers are represented in the base-ten numeration system. *(See pages 69–70.)*
a.   Identify place value names and places from hundredths through one million.
b.   Equate a number's word name, its standard form, and its expanded form.

M4N2. Students will understand and apply the concept of rounding numbers. *(See pages 71–72.)*
a.   Round numbers to the nearest ten, hundred, or thousand.
b.   Describe situations in which rounding numbers would be appropriate and determine whether to round to the nearest ten, hundred, or thousand.
c.   Understand the meaning of rounding a decimal fraction to the nearest whole number.
d.   Represent the results of computation as a rounded number when appropriate and estimate a sum or difference by rounding numbers.

M4N3. Students will solve problems involving multiplication of two- and three-digit numbers by one- and two-digit numbers. *(See page 73.)*

M4N4. Students will further develop their understanding of division of whole numbers and divide in problem-solving situations without calculators. *(See pages 74–75.)*
a.   Know the division facts with understanding and fluency.
b.   Solve problems involving division by a two-digit number (including those that generate a remainder).
c.   Understand the relationship between dividend, divisor, quotient, and remainder.
d.   Understand and explain the effect on the quotient of multiplying or dividing both the divisor and dividend by the same number. ($2{,}050 \div 50$ yields the same answer as $205 \div 5$).

M4N5. Students will further develop their understanding of the meaning of decimal fractions and use them in computations. *(See pages 76–77.)*
a.   Understand decimal fractions are a part of the base-ten system.
b.   Understand the relative size of numbers and order two-digit decimal fractions.
c.   Add and subtract both one- and two-digit decimal fractions.
d.   Model multiplication and division of decimal fractions by whole numbers.
e.   Multiply and divide both one- and two-digit decimal fractions by whole numbers.

M4N6. Students will further develop their understanding of the meaning of common fractions and use them in computations. *(See pages 78–79.)*
a.   Understand representations of simple equivalent fractions.
b.   Add and subtract fractions and mixed numbers with common denominators. (Denominators should not exceed twelve.)
c.   Convert and use mixed numbers and improper fractions interchangeably.

Number and Operations Standards

M4N7. Students will explain and use properties of the four arithmetic operations to solve and check problems. *(See pages 80–82.)*

a. Describe situations in which the four operations may be used and the relationships among them.

b. Compute using the order of operations, including parentheses.

c. Compute using the commutative, associative, and distributive properties.

d. Use mental math and estimation strategies to compute.

What it means:

- The **associative property** means the grouping of the numbers can be changed and still yield the same answer.
- The **commutative property** means the order of the numbers can be switched and still yield the same answer.
- The **distributive property** is used when there is a combination of multiplication over addition or subtraction. For example, $5 \times (3 + 6) = 5 \times 3 + 5 \times 6$.

Mathematics

| M4N1 |

Understanding Place Value

DIRECTIONS: Choose the best answer.

1. **What is the numeral for one million, three hundred fifty-two thousand, twenty-one?**

   (A) 1,352,221

   (B) 135,221

   (C) 13,520,210

   (D) 1,352,021

2. **What is the word name for 1,382,004?**

   (F) one hundred million, three hundred eighty-two thousand, four

   (G) one million, three hundred eighty-two thousand, four hundred

   (H) one hundred million, three hundred eighty-two thousand, four hundred

   (J) one million, three hundred eighty-two thousand, four

3. **What is the numeral for three million, twenty-eight thousand, fourteen?**

   (A) 3,028,014

   (B) 3,280,014

   (C) 3,028,140

   (D) 3,208,140

4. **What is the word name for 352,001?**

   (F) three hundred fifty-two thousand, one

   (G) three hundred fifty-two thousand, one hundred

   (H) three million, fifty-two thousand, one

   (J) three hundred fifty-two thousand, ten

DIRECTIONS: Build each number.

5. 5 tenths
   6 hundredths
   8 tens
   2 ones

6. 7 ones
   6 tenths
   2 tens
   1 hundredths
   3 hundreds

7. 4 hundredths
   5 tens
   4 tenths
   9 ones

8. 6 ones
   9 tens
   8 tenths
   7 hundredths

9. 0 hundreds
   3 tenths
   1 ones
   7 hundredths
   2 tens
   4 thousands

Insert the decimal point in the correct square.

STOP

Mathematics

| M4N1 |

Expanded Notation

DIRECTIONS: Choose the best answer.

 Clue Read the questions carefully. Try to think of an answer before you look at the answers.

1. **How can you write 56,890 in expanded notation?**

   (A) $5 + 6 + 8 + 9 + 0 =$

   (B) $50,000 + 6,000 + 800 + 90 =$

   (C) $56,000 + 8,900 =$

   (D) $0.5 + 0.06 + 0.008 + 0.0009 =$

2. **What is another name for 651?**

   (F) 6 thousands, 5 tens, and 1 one

   (G) 6 hundreds, 1 tens, and 5 ones

   (H) 6 tens and 5 ones

   (J) 6 hundreds, 5 tens, and 1 one

3. **What is another name for 5 hundreds and 7 thousands?**

   (A) 5,700

   (B) 7,050

   (C) 570

   (D) 7,500

4. **What is another name for 8 hundreds, 4 tens, and 3 ones?**

   (F) 8,430

   (G) 843

   (H) 834

   (J) 8,043

5. **What is another name for 4 hundreds, 6 tens, and 5 ones?**

   (A) 4,650

   (B) 465

   (C) 40,650

   (D) 4,560

6. **How can you write 9,876 in expanded notation?**

   (F) $9,800 + 76 + 0$

   (G) $9,800 + 70 + 60$

   (H) $9,000 + 870 + 60$

   (J) $9,000 + 800 + 70 + 6$

7. **What number equals $4,000 + 200 + 20 + 2$?**

   (A) 4,202

   (B) 4,200

   (C) 4,022

   (D) 4,222

8. **How can you write 10,575 in expanded notation?**

   (F) $10,000 + 50 + 70 + 5$

   (G) $10,000 + 500 + 70 + 5$

   (H) $1,000 + 500 + 70 + 5$

   (J) $100,000 + 5,000 + 700 + 5$

STOP

Mathematics

| M4N2 |

Rounding Whole Numbers

DIRECTIONS: Round to the nearest ten.

1. 16 _____

2. 75 _____

3. 27 _____

4. 23 _____

5. 32 _____

6. 92 _____

7. 54 _____

8. 95 _____

9. 58 _____

10. 82 _____

11. 66 _____

12. 48 _____

36 rounds up to 40

DIRECTIONS: Round to the nearest hundred.

13. 921 _____

14. 458 _____

15. 393 _____

16. 265 _____

17. 662 _____

18. 187 _____

19. 527 _____

20. 749 _____

21. 882 _____

22. 363 _____

23. 211 _____

24. 462 _____

DIRECTIONS: Round to nearest thousand.

25. 2,495 _____

26. 7,001 _____

27. 5,111 _____

28. 4,659 _____

29. 3,379 _____

30. 8,821 _____

31. 9,339 _____

32. 7,831 _____

33. 4,289 _____

34. 6,213 _____

35. 2,985 _____

36. 3,492 _____

STOP

Mathematics

M4N2

Rounding Decimals

DIRECTIONS: Choose the best answer.

1. **What is $73.52 rounded to the nearest dollar?**
   - (A) $73.50
   - (B) $74.00
   - (C) $73.00
   - (D) $75.00

2. **Round 3.42 to the nearest whole number.**
   - (F) 3.4
   - (G) 3.5
   - (H) 3.0
   - (J) 3.3

3. **Round 0.87 to the nearest whole number.**
   - (A) 0.9
   - (B) 0.8
   - (C) 1.0
   - (D) 0.7

4. **Round 1.15 to the nearest whole number.**
   - (F) 1.2
   - (G) 1.1
   - (H) 1.0
   - (J) 2.0

5. **Round 6.79 to the nearest whole number.**
   - (A) 6.0
   - (B) 7.0
   - (C) 6.7
   - (D) 6.8

6. **Round 5.81 to the nearest whole number.**
   - (F) 6.0
   - (G) 5.0
   - (H) 5.8
   - (J) 5.9

7. **Round 1.35 to the nearest whole number.**
   - (A) 1.4
   - (B) 1.3
   - (C) 1.0
   - (D) 2.0

8. **Round 6.98 to the nearest whole number.**
   - (F) 6.0
   - (G) 7.0
   - (H) 6.8
   - (J) 6.9

9. **Round 1.76 to the nearest whole number.**
   - (A) 1.7
   - (B) 1.6
   - (C) 1.0
   - (D) 2.0

10. **Round 3.13 to the nearest whole number.**
    - (F) 3.1
    - (G) 3.2
    - (H) 3.0
    - (J) 4.0

STOP

Mathematics

| M4N3 |

Multiplying Two- and Three-Digit Numbers

DIRECTIONS: Solve the following problems.

1.
$$\begin{array}{r} 67 \\ \times\ 8 \\ \hline \end{array}$$

2.
$$\begin{array}{r} 11 \\ \times\ 6 \\ \hline \end{array}$$

3.
$$\begin{array}{r} 74 \\ \times\ 7 \\ \hline \end{array}$$

4.
$$\begin{array}{r} 86 \\ \times\ 4 \\ \hline \end{array}$$

5.
$$\begin{array}{r} 52 \\ \times\ 8 \\ \hline \end{array}$$

6.
$$\begin{array}{r} 82 \\ \times\ 95 \\ \hline \end{array}$$

7.
$$\begin{array}{r} 53 \\ \times\ 64 \\ \hline \end{array}$$

8.
$$\begin{array}{r} 24 \\ \times\ 49 \\ \hline \end{array}$$

9.
$$\begin{array}{r} 48 \\ \times\ 89 \\ \hline \end{array}$$

10.
$$\begin{array}{r} 72 \\ \times\ 84 \\ \hline \end{array}$$

11.
$$\begin{array}{r} 351 \\ \times\ 6 \\ \hline \end{array}$$

12.
$$\begin{array}{r} 438 \\ \times\ 9 \\ \hline \end{array}$$

13.
$$\begin{array}{r} 942 \\ \times\ 2 \\ \hline \end{array}$$

14.
$$\begin{array}{r} 313 \\ \times\ 7 \\ \hline \end{array}$$

15.
$$\begin{array}{r} 946 \\ \times\ 4 \\ \hline \end{array}$$

16.
$$\begin{array}{r} 355 \\ \times\ 51 \\ \hline \end{array}$$

17.
$$\begin{array}{r} 274 \\ \times\ 32 \\ \hline \end{array}$$

18.
$$\begin{array}{r} 809 \\ \times\ 67 \\ \hline \end{array}$$

19.
$$\begin{array}{r} 456 \\ \times\ 12 \\ \hline \end{array}$$

20.
$$\begin{array}{r} 741 \\ \times\ 39 \\ \hline \end{array}$$

STOP

Mathematics

| M4N4 |

Division Facts

DIRECTIONS: Choose the best answer.

1. **144 ÷ 12 =**
   - (A) 9
   - (B) 12
   - (C) 14
   - (D) 11

2. **54 ÷ 9 =**
   - (F) 4
   - (G) 5
   - (H) 6
   - (J) 7

3. **36 ÷ 6 =**
   - (A) 13
   - (B) 3
   - (C) 12
   - (D) 6

4. **132 ÷ 11 =**
   - (F) 10
   - (G) 11
   - (H) 12
   - (J) 13

5. **18 ÷ 2 =**
   - (A) 9
   - (B) 6
   - (C) 8
   - (D) 7

6. **110 ÷ 10 =**
   - (F) 9
   - (G) 10
   - (H) 11
   - (J) 12

7. **81 ÷ 9 =**
   - (A) 9
   - (B) 7
   - (C) 8
   - (D) 6

8. **60 ÷ 5 =**
   - (F) 11
   - (G) 9
   - (H) 12
   - (J) 10

9. **56 ÷ 8 =**
   - (A) 7
   - (B) 5
   - (C) 6
   - (D) 8

10. **24 ÷ 6 =**
    - (F) 3
    - (G) 4
    - (H) 5
    - (J) 6

11. **72 ÷ 8 =**
    - (A) 6
    - (B) 7
    - (C) 8
    - (D) 9

12. **121 ÷ 11 =**
    - (F) 9
    - (G) 10
    - (H) 11
    - (J) 12

STOP

Mathematics

| M4N4 |

Division

DIRECTIONS: Find the following quotients. Several problems will have remainders. Show all of your work.

1. 6)372

2. 4)19

3. 5)845

4. 12)780

5. 7)45

6. 11)165

7. 8)26

8. 5)28

9. 20)580

10. 24)960

11. 3)26

12. 7)798

13. 2)19

14. 6)51

15. 3)639

STOP

Mathematics

| M4N5 |

Comparing and Ordering Decimals

DIRECTIONS: Choose the best answer.

1. **Which decimal below names the smallest number?**
   - (A) 0.06
   - (B) 0.6
   - (C) 0.64
   - (D) 6.40

2. **Which decimal below names the largest number?**
   - (F) 2.15
   - (G) 2.05
   - (H) 2.50
   - (J) 2.21

3. **What is the correct sign to complete the equation $426.10 ▨ $416.19?**
   - (A) =
   - (B) <
   - (C) >
   - (D) none of these

4. **Which decimal below names the smallest number?**
   - (F) 1.90
   - (G) 1.21
   - (H) 1.09
   - (J) 1.18

5. **Which group of numbers is in order from smallest to largest?**
   - (A) 21.09, 21.9, 21.98, 22.01, 22.10
   - (B) 21.09, 21.98, 21.9, 22.10, 22.01
   - (C) 21.98, 21.09, 21.9, 22.10, 22.01
   - (D) 21.9, 21.09, 21.98, 22.10, 22.01

6. **Which group of numbers is in order from greatest to least?**
   - (F) 0.99, 0.95, 0.59, 0.05, 0.09
   - (G) 0.09, 0.05, 0.59, 0.99, 0.95
   - (H) 0.99, 0.95, 0.59, 0.09, 0.05
   - (J) 0.95, 0.99, 0.59, 0.05, 0.09

7. **What is the correct sign to complete the equation 18.58 ▨ 18.85?**
   - (A) =
   - (B) <
   - (C) >
   - (D) none of these

8. **Which decimal below names the largest number?**
   - (F) 3.17
   - (G) 3.07
   - (H) 3.71
   - (J) 3.10

STOP

Mathematics

| M4N5 |

Decimal Computations

DIRECTIONS: Find the answers to the following addition and subtraction number sentences.

1. $4.2 + 5.2 =$ _____

2. $6.4 + 1.5 =$ _____

3. $3.1 + 7.8 =$ _____

4. $4.7 + 3.2 =$ _____

5. $4.9 + 2.0 =$ _____

6. $5.9 - 3.2 =$ _____

7. $6.7 - 5.6 =$ _____

8. $7.8 - 2.5 =$ _____

9. $5.8 - 3.3 =$ _____

10. $3.9 - 1.5 =$ _____

11. $0.23 + 0.25 =$ _____

12. $0.43 + 0.16 =$ _____

13. $0.26 + 0.42 =$ _____

14. $0.64 + 0.15 =$ _____

15. $0.68 - 0.31 =$ _____

16. $5.34 - 2.43 =$ _____

DIRECTIONS: Find the answers to the following multiplication and division number sentences.

17. $39.3 \div 3 =$ _____

18. $9.8 \times 5 =$ _____

19. $22.3 \times 8 =$ _____

20. $48.4 \div 4 =$ _____

21. $76.5 \div 5 =$ _____

22. $5.3 \times 4 =$ _____

23. $72.8 \div 4 =$ _____

24. $54.9 \div 9 =$ _____

25. $56.7 \times 6 =$ _____

26. $15.7 \times 4 =$ _____

27. $62.3 \times 3 =$ _____

28. $24.8 \div 4 =$ _____

29. $12.8 \div 8 =$ _____

30. $40.6 \times 7 =$ _____

31. $6.2 \times 10 =$ _____

32. $36.8 \div 4 =$ _____

STOP

Mathematics

M4N6

Identifying
Equivalent Fractions

DIRECTIONS: Add the missing numbers to make equivalent fractions.

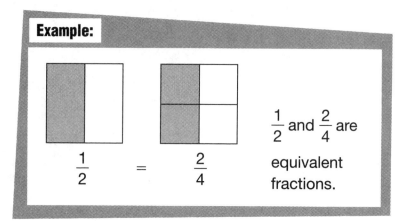

Example:

$\dfrac{1}{2}$ = $\dfrac{2}{4}$

$\dfrac{1}{2}$ and $\dfrac{2}{4}$ are equivalent fractions.

 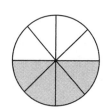

1. $\dfrac{2}{4}$ = $\dfrac{}{8}$

 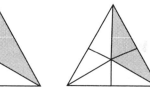

2. $\dfrac{1}{3}$ = $\dfrac{}{}$

 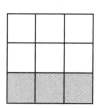

3. $\dfrac{1}{3}$ = $\dfrac{}{}$

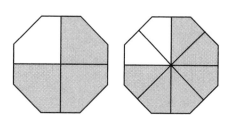

4. $\dfrac{3}{4}$ = $\dfrac{}{}$

5. $\dfrac{1}{4}$ = $\dfrac{}{16}$

6. $\dfrac{1}{2}$ = $\dfrac{}{8}$

7. $\dfrac{1}{3}$ = $\dfrac{}{9}$

8. $\dfrac{2}{3}$ = $\dfrac{}{15}$

9. $\dfrac{2}{3}$ = $\dfrac{}{12}$

10. $\dfrac{1}{2}$ = $\dfrac{}{10}$

STOP

Name _____ Date _____

Mathematics

Number and Operations

Adding and Subtracting Fractions

DIRECTIONS: Choose the correct answer to each equation in simplest form. Choose "none of these" if the correct answer is not given.

Examples:

$\frac{4}{5} + \frac{4}{5} =$

- Ⓐ $\frac{5}{8}$
- Ⓑ $1\frac{3}{5}$
- Ⓒ 1
- Ⓓ none of these

Answer: Ⓑ

$1\frac{4}{7}$
$- \frac{3}{7}$

- Ⓕ 2
- Ⓖ $1\frac{1}{7}$
- Ⓗ $\frac{17}{7}$
- Ⓙ none of these

Answer: Ⓖ

Clue

Look closely at the operation sign. Add whole numbers together first, then fractions. Remember to reduce to simplest form.

---

1. $2\frac{1}{5}$
    $+ 1\frac{3}{5}$

    - Ⓐ 4
    - Ⓑ $3\frac{4}{5}$
    - Ⓒ $3\frac{2}{5}$
    - Ⓓ none of these

2. $\frac{3}{4} - \frac{1}{4} =$

    - Ⓕ $\frac{4}{4}$
    - Ⓖ 1
    - Ⓗ $\frac{1}{2}$
    - Ⓙ none of these

3. $\frac{1}{10} + \frac{5}{10} =$

    - Ⓐ $\frac{10}{6}$
    - Ⓑ $\frac{4}{5}$
    - Ⓒ $\frac{6}{10}$
    - Ⓓ none of these

4. $\frac{5}{8} + \frac{7}{8} + \frac{1}{8} =$

    - Ⓕ $1\frac{3}{8}$
    - Ⓖ $1\frac{3}{24}$
    - Ⓗ $1\frac{5}{8}$
    - Ⓙ none of these

5. $\frac{6}{6} - \frac{6}{6} =$

    - Ⓐ 0
    - Ⓑ $\frac{12}{6}$
    - Ⓒ $\frac{0}{6}$
    - Ⓓ none of these

6. $\blacksquare - \frac{2}{9} = \frac{5}{9}$

    - Ⓕ $1\frac{1}{9}$
    - Ⓖ $\frac{3}{9}$
    - Ⓗ $\frac{7}{9}$
    - Ⓙ none of these

STOP

Solving Multi-Step Problems

DIRECTIONS: Choose the best answer.

Clue   Remember the order of operations: parentheses, multiplication, division,
addition, and subtraction.

1. **Find 3 + (51 ÷ 3).**
   - (A) 17
   - (B) 20
   - (C) 57
   - (D) 54

2. **Find (2 × 1,000) + (6 × 100) + (9 × 1).**
   - (F) 2,690
   - (G) 2,609
   - (H) 269
   - (J) 2,069

3. **Find (8 × 2) + 4.**
   - (A) 10
   - (B) 14
   - (C) 20
   - (D) 23

4. **Find 3 × (4 + 1).**
   - (F) 13
   - (G) 15
   - (H) 9
   - (J) 16

5. **Find (3 × 4) + 1.**
   - (A) 13
   - (B) 15
   - (C) 9
   - (D) 16

6. **Find 5 + (2 × 3) − 2.**
   - (F) 19
   - (G) 13
   - (H) 11
   - (J) 9

7. **Find (4 × 2) + (3 × 3).**
   - (A) 17
   - (B) 12
   - (C) 23
   - (D) 60

8. **Find 1 + (5 × 4) + 2.**
   - (F) 26
   - (G) 23
   - (H) 21
   - (J) 60

9. **Find 2 × (278 + 3).**
   - (A) 562
   - (B) 281
   - (C) 559
   - (D) 1,668

10. **Find (4 × 4) + (7 × 3) + (8 − 2).**
   - (F) 27
   - (G) 43
   - (H) 39
   - (J) 37

STOP

Mathematics

M4N7

Commutative and Associative Properties

Examples:

The **commutative property** says you can switch the order of the numbers and still get the same answer.

$$5 + 10 = 10 + 5 \qquad 5 \times 2 = 2 \times 5$$
$$15 = 15 \qquad\qquad 10 = 10$$

The **associative property** says you can change the grouping of the numbers and still get the same answer.

$$(3 + 5) + 6 = 3 + (5 + 6) \qquad (3 \times 5) \times 6 = 3 \times (5 \times 6)$$
$$8 + 6 = 3 + 11 \qquad\qquad 15 \times 6 = 3 \times 30$$
$$14 = 14 \qquad\qquad\qquad 90 = 90$$

DIRECTIONS: Identify the property that makes each of these number sentences true. Write **A** for the associative property or **C** for the commutative property.

_____ 1. $59 + 43 = 43 + 59$

_____ 2. $(7 + 8) + 6 = 7 + (8 + 6)$

_____ 3. $(5 + 2) + 3 = 3 + (5 + 2)$

_____ 4. $5 \times (8 \times 6) = (5 \times 8) \times 6$

_____ 5. $3 \times 2 = 2 \times 3$

_____ 6. $412 \times (13 \times 15) = 412 \times (15 \times 13)$

DIRECTIONS: Rewrite each of the expressions in an equivalent form, using the property indicated.

7. $4 \times 3 =$ _____ **commutative**

8. $5 + 8 + 6 =$ _____ **commutative**

9. $7 \times (4 \times 3) =$ _____ **associative**

10. $7 \times (4 \times 3) =$ _____ **commutative**

11. $(8 + 4) + 2 =$ _____ **associative**

12. $(8 + 4) + 2 =$ _____ **commutative**

STOP

Mathematics

Distributive Property

Number and Operations

DIRECTIONS: Use the **distributive property** to rewrite the following expressions. Then, use the correct order of operations to solve both sides and check your answers.

Example:

The **distributive property** is used when there is a combination of multiplication over addition or subtraction.

$$5(3 + 6) = 5 \times 3 + 5 \times 6$$
$$5 \times 9 = 15 + 30$$
$$45 = 45$$

$$16 - 6 = (8 \times 2) - (3 \times 2)$$
$$10 = (8 - 3)2$$
$$10 = 10$$

1. $2(6 + 3) =$

2. $12 + 9 =$

3. $4(9 - 1) =$

4. $18 - 6 =$

5. $(15 - 3)2 =$

6. $(7 + 5)8 =$

7. $25 - 15 =$

8. $3(5 + 6) =$

9. $8 + 12 =$

Mathematics

| M4N1–M4N7 |

For pages 69–82

Mini-Test 1

DIRECTIONS: Choose the best answer.

1. **What is the numeral for four million, eight hundred two thousand, sixteen?**
   - (A) 4,802,160
   - (B) 4,082,016
   - (C) 4,802,016
   - (D) 4,802,160

2. **Fifty-three hundredths is the same as _____ .**
   - (F) 5,300
   - (G) 530
   - (H) 0.53
   - (J) 0.053

3. **How can you write 43,985 in expanded notation?**
   - (A) 43,000 + 900 + 85
   - (B) 40,000 + 3,000 + 900 + 80 + 5
   - (C) 43,000 + 900 + 80 + 5
   - (D) 40,000 + 390 + 80 + 5

4. **What is 793 rounded to the nearest hundred?**
   - (F) 700
   - (G) 780
   - (H) 800
   - (J) 790

5. **Round 2.86 to the nearest whole number.**
   - (A) 2.8
   - (B) 3.0
   - (C) 2.0
   - (D) 2.9

6. **178 × 84 =**
   - (F) 262
   - (G) 94
   - (H) 14,952
   - (J) 1,424

7. **72 ÷ 9 =**
   - (A) 9
   - (B) 7
   - (C) 8
   - (D) 6

8. **435 ÷ 15 =**
   - (F) 30
   - (G) 29
   - (H) 27
   - (J) 28

9. **33 ÷ 7 =**
   - (A) 4 R2
   - (B) 5 R3
   - (C) 4 R8
   - (D) 4 R5

10. **Which decimal below names the smallest number?**
    - (F) 0.28
    - (G) 2.08
    - (H) 0.08
    - (J) 0.82

11. **6.5 + 3.8 =**
    - (A) 2.7
    - (B) 10.1
    - (C) 10.3
    - (D) 9.3

GO

12. 7.5 − 3.1 =

- (F) 5.4
- (G) 4.4
- (H) 10.6
- (J) 2.4

13. 16.8 ÷ 2 =

- (A) 8.4
- (B) 9.4
- (C) 4.2
- (D) 8

14. 6.3 × 8 =

- (F) 48.3
- (G) 48
- (H) 50.8
- (J) 50.4

15. $\dfrac{3}{12}$ =

- (A) $\dfrac{3}{4}$
- (C) $\dfrac{2}{6}$
- (B) $\dfrac{1}{6}$
- (D) $\dfrac{1}{4}$

16. $2\dfrac{4}{8}$

$+ \ \dfrac{3}{8}$

- (F) 3
- (H) $2\dfrac{7}{8}$
- (G) $2\dfrac{1}{8}$
- (J) $2\dfrac{1}{4}$

17. $\dfrac{7}{9}$

$- \ \dfrac{6}{9}$

- (A) $1\dfrac{4}{9}$
- (C) $\dfrac{13}{9}$
- (B) $\dfrac{1}{9}$
- (D) $\dfrac{1}{3}$

18. Find (4 × 5) + 23.

- (F) 31
- (G) 43
- (H) 3
- (J) 40

19. Find [4 + (2 × 13)] ÷ 5.

- (A) 35
- (B) 5
- (C) 15
- (D) 6

20. The following number sentence is an example of which property?

$$(7 \times 3) \times 2 = 7 \times (3 \times 2)$$

- (F) commutative
- (G) associative
- (H) distributive
- (J) none of these

21. The following number sentence is an example of which property?

$$4 + 5 = 5 + 4$$

- (A) commutative
- (B) associative
- (C) distributive
- (D) none of these

22. The following number sentence is an example of which property?

$$7(3 + 8) = (7 \times 3) + (7 \times 8)$$

- (F) commutative
- (G) associative
- (H) distributive
- (J) none of these

STOP

Measurement Standards

M4M. Measurement
Students will measure weight in appropriate metric and standard units. They will also measure angles.

M4M1. Students will understand the concept of weight and how to measure it. *(See pages 86–87.)*
a. Use standard and metric units to measure the weight of objects.
b. Know units used to measure weight (gram, kilogram, ounces, pounds, and tons).
c. Compare one unit to another within a single system of measurement.

M4M2. Students will understand the concept of angles and how to measure them. *(See pages 88–89.)*
a. Use tools, such as a protractor or angle ruler, and other methods such as paper folding, drawing a diagonal in a square, to measure angles.
b. Understand the meaning and measure of a half rotation (180°) and a full rotation (360°).

Mathematics

M4M1

Customary
Units of Weight

DIRECTIONS: Find the following conversions. Below is a chart of weight conversions. Use the chart to help you figure the conversions.

1 pound (lb.) = 16 ounces (oz.)
1 ton (t.) = 2,000 pounds (lbs.)

1 TON

1. 2 lbs. = _____ oz.

2. 160 oz. = _____ lbs.

3. 15 lbs. = _____ oz.

4. 16,000 lbs. = _____ t.

5. 10 lbs. = _____ oz.

6. 5,000 lbs. = _____ t.

7. 6 t. = _____ lbs.

8. 20 lbs. = _____ oz.

9. 64 oz. = _____ lbs.

DIRECTIONS: Read the following problems and answer the questions.

10. Kwaku has a 2-pound bag of soil. How many ounces is the bag?

   _____

11. A young rhino weighs 2,500 pounds. How many tons is the rhino?

   _____

12. A particular bridge has a weight capacity of 15 tons. A truck's loaded trailer weighs 40,000 pounds. Should the trucker drive over the bridge?

   _____

13. A recipe for apple pie calls for 2 pounds of apples. The produce scale says 34 ounces. Are there enough apples for a pie?

   _____

Name _____   Date _____

Mathematics   **Measurement**

Metric
Units of Weight

DIRECTIONS: Find the following conversions. Below is a chart of metric conversions. Use the chart to help you figure the conversions.

> 1 gram (g) = 1,000 milligrams (mg)
> 1 kilogram (kg) = 1,000 grams (g)
> 1 decagram (dag) = 10 kilograms (kg)
> 1 hectogram (hg) = 100 kilograms (kg)
> 1 metric ton (t) = 1,000 kilograms (kg)

1. 10 kg = _____ g

2. 1 hg = _____ dag

3. 2,000 g = _____ kg

4. 500 g = _____ kg

5. 70 hg = _____ t

6. 2 g = _____ mg

7. 3 t = _____ kg

8. 4,500 g = _____ kg

9. 30 kg = _____ dag

10. 6,000 mg = _____ g

11. 4 dag = _____ kg

12. 500 kg = _____ hg

DIRECTIONS: Read the following problems and answer the questions.

13. Emilio has a bag of polished stones, each with a weight of 200 grams. How many stones are in the bag if the total weight equals 2 kilograms? _____

14. Tasha has a jar full of cookies with a weight of 175 grams. Each cookie weighs 5 grams. How many cookies are in the jar? _____

15. Kara has a collection of objects. Her plastic spider ring has a weight of 980 milligrams. A piece of quartz has a weight of 3 grams and a bag of buttons has a weight of 2,020 milligrams. What is the total weight of her collection in grams? _____

16. When Mark placed the green grapes on the scale, the weight was 200 grams short of 1 kilogram. He placed another 500 grams on the scale and decided to buy the whole bunch. How many grams in all did he purchase? _____

Mathematics   **Measurement**

M4M2   # Measuring Angles

DIRECTIONS: Use a protractor or angle ruler to measure the following angles.

1. _____

2. _____

3. _____

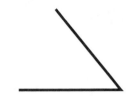

4. _____

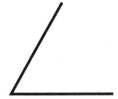

5. _____

6. _____

7. _____

8. _____

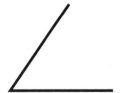

9. _____

STOP

Name _____ Date _____

Mathematics   Measurement

M4M2   # Understanding Rotation

DIRECTIONS: The size of an angle is measured in many ways. One method is to use degrees. The degrees tell you how far you rotated to make the angle. Think of the minute hand on a clock. In one hour, the hand sweeps around in one full circle, ending back where it started. It has made one full turn, which equals 360 degrees, or 360°. This chart shows angles measured by the rotation of a circle, the minutes on a clock, and degrees. Use it to help you with the questions below.

Rotation	Minutes	Degrees
$\frac{1}{4}$ turn	15	90
$\frac{1}{2}$ turn	30	180
$\frac{3}{4}$ turn	45	270
full turn	60	360

For each problem, write the degree measure of the angle made when the minute hand on a clock travels from the first time to the second time.

1. 3:15 to 3:30   **90°**

2. 7:45 to 8:15   _____

3. 4:15 to 5:15   _____

4. 2:00 to 2:45   _____

5. 6:30 to 7:00   _____

6. 11:15 to 11:30   _____

7. 9:30 to 10:00   _____

8. 5:45 to 6:30   _____

9. 4:15 to 5:00   _____

10. 1:30 to 2:00   _____

11. 8:45 to 9:00   _____

12. 4:25 to 4:40   _____

13. 9:30 to 10:30   _____

14. 3:30 to 3:45   _____

15. 4:20 to 4:50   _____

16. 7:03 to 7:48   _____

17. 5:10 to 5:25   _____

18. 2:15 to 2:30   _____

19. 6:04 to 6:49   _____

20. 7:48 to 8:48   _____

STOP

Mathematics

| M4M1–M4M2 |

Mini-Test 2

For pages 86–89

DIRECTIONS: Choose the best answer.

1. **A truck has 6 tons of cargo. How many pounds is that?**
   - (A) 12,000 pounds
   - (B) 1,200 pounds
   - (C) 120 pounds
   - (D) 12 pounds

2. **9 kilograms is how many grams?**
   - (F) 90,000 grams
   - (G) 90 grams
   - (H) 900 grams
   - (J) 9,000 grams

3. **Deann bought a 5-pound bag of flour. How many ounces is the bag?**
   - (A) 80 ounces
   - (B) 60 ounces
   - (C) 24 ounces
   - (D) 32 ounces

4. **Becky weighs 48,000 grams. How many kilograms is this?**
   - (F) 480 kilograms
   - (G) 4.8 kilograms
   - (H) 48 kilograms
   - (J) 4,800 kilograms

5. **A 180° angle shows how much of a turn?**
   - (A) $\frac{1}{4}$ turn
   - (B) $\frac{1}{2}$ turn
   - (C) $\frac{3}{4}$ turn
   - (D) full turn

6. **A 360° angle shows how much of a turn?**
   - (F) $\frac{1}{4}$ turn
   - (G) $\frac{1}{2}$ turn
   - (H) $\frac{3}{4}$ turn
   - (J) full turn

7. **What is the degree measure of the angle made when the minute hand on a clock travels from 2:25 to 3:10?**
   - (A) 90°
   - (B) 180°
   - (C) 270°
   - (D) 360°

STOP

Geometry Standards

M4G. Geometry

Students will understand and construct plane and solid geometric figures. They will also graph points on the coordinate plane.

M4G1. Students will define and identify the characteristics of geometric figures through examination and construction. *(See pages 92–94.)*

a. Examine and compare angles in order to classify and identify triangles by their angles.

b. Describe parallel and perpendicular lines in plane geometric figures.

c. Examine and classify quadrilaterals (including parallelograms, squares, rectangles, trapezoids, and rhombi).

d. Compare and contrast the relationships among quadrilaterals.

What it means:

● Two lines in a plane are **parallel** if they never cross; two lines or planes are **perpendicular** to each other if the angle between them is 90 degrees, or a right angle.

M4G2. Students will understand fundamental solid figures. *(See pages 95–96.)*

a. Compare and contrast a cube and a rectangular prism in terms of the number and shape of their faces, edges, and vertices.

b. Describe parallel and perpendicular lines and planes in connection with the rectangular prism.

c. Construct/collect models for solid geometric figures (cube, prisms, cylinder, etc.).

What it means:

● The **faces** of a figure are the flat surfaces. The **vertices** of a figure are the corners. The **edges** are the lines where the surfaces meet.

M4G3. Students will use the coordinate system. *(See pages 97–98.)*

a. Understand and apply ordered pairs in the first quadrant of the coordinate system.

b. Locate a point in the first quadrant in the coordinate plane and name the ordered pair.

c. Graph ordered pairs in the first quadrant.

Mathematics   **Geometry**

Identifying
Triangles Using Angles

DIRECTIONS: Follow the instructions for each type of triangle. Remember, triangles can be more than one type.

Right Triangle—One of the angles measures 90 degrees (an *L*-shaped angle).
Acute Triangle—All angles in the triangle measure less than 90 degrees.
Obtuse Triangle—One of the angles measures more than 90 degrees.

- Color all the **right** triangles blue.
- Color all the **acute** triangles red.
- Color all the **obtuse** triangles green.

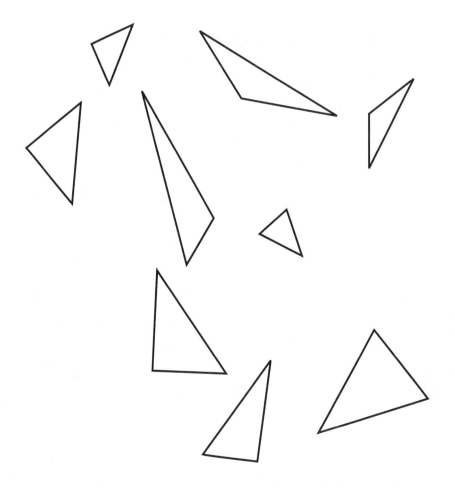

Name _____ Date _____

Parallel and
Perpendicular Lines

Clue Two lines in a plane are **parallel** if they never cross. Two lines are **perpendicular** if the angle between them is 90°, or a right angle.

DIRECTIONS: Choose the best answer.

1. **These lines are _____ .**
   - (A) parallel
   - (B) perpendicular
   - (C) right
   - (D) none of the above

2. **These lines are _____ .**
   - (F) obtuse
   - (G) perpendicular
   - (H) parallel
   - (J) none of the above

3. **These lines are _____ .**
   - (A) parallel
   - (B) perpendicular
   - (C) obtuse
   - (D) none of the above

4. **These lines are _____ .**
   - (F) right
   - (G) perpendicular
   - (H) parallel
   - (J) none of the above

5. **These lines are _____ .**
   - (A) parallel
   - (B) perpendicular
   - (C) obtuse
   - (D) none of the above

DIRECTIONS: Use the square below for questions 6–7.

6. **In the square above, sides A and B and sides C and D are _____ .**
   - (F) parallel
   - (G) perpendicular
   - (H) obtuse
   - (J) none of the above

7. **In the square above, sides A and C and sides B and D are _____ .**
   - (A) parallel
   - (B) perpendicular
   - (C) obtuse
   - (D) none of the above

8. **In the figure below, which sides are perpendicular?**
   - (F) A and C
   - (G) A and B
   - (H) D and B
   - (J) None of the sides are perpendicular.

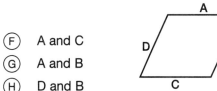

Name _____ Date _____

Mathematics

| M4G1 |

Geometry

Identifying Quadrilaterals

DIRECTIONS: Classify the shapes below as **quadrilateral**, **trapezoid**, **parallelogram**, **rectangle**, **square**, or **rhombus**.

A **quadrilateral** is any figure with 4 sides and 4 angles. Some quadrilaterals have special names.

Trapezoid—a quadrilateral with 1 set of parallel sides

Parallelogram—a quadrilateral with 2 sets of parallel sides

Rectangle—a quadrilateral with 4 right angles and opposite sides of equal length

Square—a quadrilateral with 4 right angles and 4 equal sides

Rhombus—a quadrilateral with 4 equal sides and 2 pairs of parallel sides

1.

_____

2.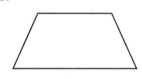

_____

3.

_____

4.

_____

5.

_____

6.

_____

7.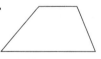

_____

8.

_____

STOP

Name _____   Date _____

Mathematics

Cubes and
Rectangular Prisms

Clue   The **faces** of a figure are the flat surfaces. The **vertices** of a figure are the
corners. The **edges** are the lines where the surfaces meet.

DIRECTIONS: Use the cube to answer questions 1–3.

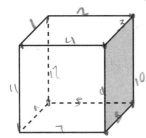

1. How many faces does the cube have?

- (A) 3
- (B) 4
- (C) 5
- (D) 6

2. How many edges does the cube have?

- (F) 10
- (G) 12
- (H) 14
- (J) 16

3. How many vertices does the cube have?

- (A) 6
- (B) 8
- (C) 10
- (D) 12

DIRECTIONS: Use the rectangular prism to answer
questions 4–6.

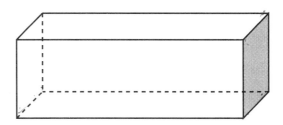

**4. How many faces does the rectangular prism
have?**

- (A) 3
- (B) 4
- (C) 5
- (D) 6

**5. How many edges does the rectangular prism
have?**

- (F) 10
- (G) 12
- (H) 14
- (J) 16

**6. How many vertices does the rectangular
prism have?**

- (A) 6
- (B) 8
- (C) 10
- (D) 12

STOP

Name _____ Date _____

Mathematics   **Geometry**

M4G2

Identifying Solid Geometric Figures

Examples:

A **cone** is a three-dimensional shape with a circular base, a curved surface, and one point, or vertex.

A **cylinder** is a three-dimensional shape with two circular bases and a curved surface.

A **sphere** is a completely curved three-dimensional shape.

DIRECTIONS: Many everyday objects contain these shapes. For each object shown below, write *cone, cylinder, sphere,* or *none of these.*

1.

_____

2.

_____

3.

_____

4.

_____

5.

_____

6.

_____

7.

_____

8.

_____

9.

_____

10.

_____

11.

_____

12.

_____

Mathematics   **Geometry**

M4G3   # Using Coordinates

DIRECTIONS: The students in Room 14 are going on a scavenger hunt at Willow Lake. Each team needs to find the objects below. Give the item from the word list that is found at each coordinate.

 Clue   Remember that the first number of an ordered pair is the number on the *x*-axis.

Word List

acorn

bird

boat

butterfly

fish

flower

frog

leaf

lily pad

picnic basket

rock

worm

1. _____ (6, 1)   7. _____ (5, 4)

2. _____ (4, 2)   8. _____ (3, 5)

3. _____ (2, 3)   9. _____ (2, 6)

4. _____ (3, 3)   10. _____ (6, 6)

5. _____ (0, 4)   11. _____ (1, 7)

6. _____ (1, 4)   12. _____ (5, 7)

DIRECTIONS: After the scavenger hunt, the students will have a picnic. Help them get ready for the picnic by drawing the given shapes at each coordinate.

13. **banana (0, 0)**   15. **milk carton (3, 4)**

14. **sandwich (7, 7)**   16. **carrot (0, 7)**

GO

DIRECTIONS: Plot the ordered pairs on the graph.
Connect the points in the order given.

18. **What shape did you make?**

- Ⓐ triangle
- Ⓑ stop sign
- Ⓒ evergreen tree
- Ⓓ car

17.

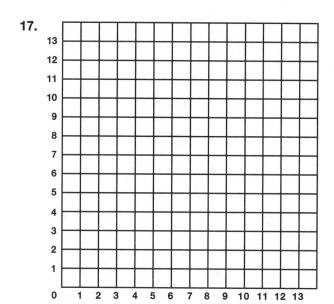

(6, 11)

(4, 9)

(5, 9)

(3, 7)

(4, 7)

(2, 5)

(3, 5)

(1, 3)

(5, 3)

(5, 1)

(7, 1)

(7, 3)

(11, 3)

(9, 5)

(10, 5)

(8, 7)

(9, 7)

(7, 9)

(8, 9)

(6, 11)

19.

(1, 0)

(3, 0)

(3, 3)

(5, 4)

(6, 6)

(6, 7)

(5, 9)

(3, 10)

(1, 10)

(1, 8)

(1, 6)

(1, 4)

(1, 2)

(1, 0)

20. **What letter did you make?**

- Ⓕ P
- Ⓖ R
- Ⓗ Q
- Ⓙ T

STOP

Name _____   Date _____

| M4G1–M4G3 |

Mini-Test 3

For pages 92–98

DIRECTIONS: Choose the best answer.

1. What type of triangle is shown?

- (A) acute
- (B) obtuse
- (C) right
- (D) none of these

2. These lines are _____ .

- (F) parallel
- (G) perpendicular
- (H) right
- (J) none of the above

3. A quadrilateral has _____ .

- (A) 3 sides
- (B) 4 sides
- (C) 5 sides
- (D) 6 sides

4. Which of the figures below is a cube?

- (F)
- (G)
- (H)
- (J)

5. How many vertices does this triangular pyramid have?

- (A) 4
- (B) 5
- (C) 6
- (D) 8

6. What is the name of this object?

- (F) pyramid
- (G) sphere
- (H) cylinder
- (J) cone

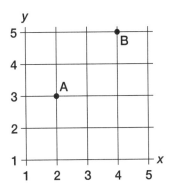

7. What are the coordinates for point A?

- (A) (3, 2)
- (B) (4, 5)
- (C) (2, 3)
- (D) (5, 4)

8. What are the coordinates for point B?

- (F) (3, 2)
- (G) (4, 5)
- (H) (2, 3)
- (J) (5, 4)

STOP

Algebra Standards

M4A. Algebra

Students will investigate and represent mathematical relationships between quantities using mathematical expressions in problem-solving situations.

M4A1. Students will represent and interpret mathematical relationships in quantitative expressions. *(See pages 101–102.)*

a. Understand and apply patterns and rules to describe relationships and solve problems.

b. Represent unknowns using symbols, such as ■ and ▲.

c. Write and evaluate mathematical expressions using symbols and different values.

Mathematics   **Algebra**

M4A1

Finding Missing
Numbers in Patterns

DIRECTIONS: Find the pattern in each row of numbers. Fill in the missing number and explain the rule for each pattern.

1. 1, 2, 3, 5, 8, 13, _____ , 34

    Rule: _____

    _____

    _____

2. 4, 5, 7, 10, 14, 19, 25, _____

    Rule: _____

    _____

    _____

3. 80, 77, 71, _____ , 50, 35, 17

    Rule: _____

    _____

    _____

4. 20, 21, 19, 22, 18, 23, _____ , 24

    Rule: _____

    _____

    _____

5. 12, 23, _____ , 89, 177, 353, 705

    Rule: _____

    _____

    _____

6. 4, 8, 16, 28, _____ , 64, 88, 116

    Rule: _____

    _____

    _____

7. _____ , 88, 86, 83, 79, 74, 68, 61

    Rule: _____

    _____

    _____

8. 15, 17, 21, 27, 35, 45, 57, _____

    Rule: _____

    _____

    _____

9. 56, 53, 55, 52, 54, _____ , 53, 50

    Rule: _____

    _____

    _____

10. 76, 81, 73, _____ , 70, 75, 67, 72

    Rule: _____

    _____

    _____

STOP

Mathematics

| M4A1 |

Using Symbols

DIRECTIONS: Choose the best answer.

1. **What number makes this number sentence true?** ■ × 4 = 8
   - Ⓐ 1
   - Ⓑ 2
   - Ⓒ 0
   - Ⓓ 4

2. **What number makes this number sentence true?** ■ × ■ = 9
   - Ⓕ 0
   - Ⓖ 2
   - Ⓗ 3
   - Ⓙ 4

3. **What number makes this number sentence true?** ■ ÷ 2 = 7
   - Ⓐ 9
   - Ⓑ 5
   - Ⓒ 3
   - Ⓓ 14

4. **What number makes this number sentence true?** ■ − 37 = 53
   - Ⓕ 100
   - Ⓖ 110
   - Ⓗ 90
   - Ⓙ 89

5. **What number makes this number sentence true?** ■ ÷ 4 = 51
   - Ⓐ 204
   - Ⓑ 240
   - Ⓒ 47
   - Ⓓ 55

Clue — To solve two-variable equations, substitute the given value for x and evaluate the equation to get y.

DIRECTIONS: Choose the best answer. For numbers 6–9, let $y = 5x + 8$.

6. **What is y when x is 2?**
   - Ⓕ 15
   - Ⓖ 13
   - Ⓗ 18
   - Ⓙ 21

7. **What is y when x is 3?**
   - Ⓐ 23
   - Ⓑ 7
   - Ⓒ 16
   - Ⓓ 8

8. **What is y when x is 5?**
   - Ⓕ 18
   - Ⓖ 17
   - Ⓗ 2
   - Ⓙ 33

9. **What is y when x is 10?**
   - Ⓐ 23
   - Ⓑ 58
   - Ⓒ 7
   - Ⓓ 18

STOP

Mathematics

M4A1

Algebra

Mini-Test 4

For pages 101–102

DIRECTIONS: Choose the best answer.

1. **What number is missing from the sequence?**

37	31		22	19

- (A) 24
- (B) 25
- (C) 26
- (D) 27

2. **Extend the following pattern and write the rule for the pattern.**

   1, 2, 4, 8, 16, _____ , _____ , _____ , _____ , _____

   Rule: _____

3. **Create a pattern of eight numbers. Start with the number 56 and add 7 to each number.**

   _____

   _____

4. **John has 13 marbles, 5 of which are a solid color. How many marbles are multicolored?**

- (F) $5 + \blacksquare = 13$
- (G) $13 + 5 = \blacksquare$
- (H) $\blacksquare - 5 = 13$
- (J) $\blacksquare + 13 = 5$

5. **What number makes this number sentence true?**

   $$56 \div \blacksquare = 7$$

- (A) 7
- (B) 5
- (C) 8
- (D) 9

6. **What number makes this number sentence true?**

   $$\blacksquare + 17 = 279$$

- (F) 262
- (G) 296
- (H) 272
- (J) 266

DIRECTIONS: For numbers 7–9, let $y = 19 - 2x$.

7. **What is y when x is 3?**

- (A) 25
- (B) 13
- (C) 17
- (D) 10

8. **What is y when x is 5?**

- (F) 9
- (G) 17
- (H) 24
- (J) 26

9. **What is y when x is 7?**

- (A) 10
- (B) 28
- (C) 33
- (D) 5

STOP

Data Analysis Standards

M4D. Data Analysis
Students will gather, organize, and display data. They will also compare features of graphs.

M4D1. Students will gather, organize, and display data according to the situation and compare related features. *(See pages 105–106.)*

a. Represent data in bar, line, and pictographs.
b. Investigate the features and tendencies of graphs.
c. Compare different graphical representations for a given set of data.

Mathematics

Data Analysis

M4D1

Interpreting Graphs

DIRECTIONS: Use the bar graph below for numbers 1–3.

Top Countries Generating Hydroelectric Power

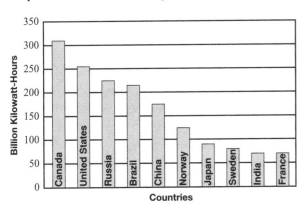

1. **Which of the following countries produces the least amount of hydroelectricity?**

   (A) Brazil

   (B) China

   (C) India

   (D) Canada

2. **Which country produces more hydroelectricity than Brazil and less than the United States?**

   (F) Russia

   (G) China

   (H) Canada

   (J) Brazil

3. **Which two countries produce about the same amount of hydroelectricity?**

   (A) India and France

   (B) Russia and Brazil

   (C) Japan and Sweden

   (D) Sweden and India

DIRECTIONS: Use the pictograph below for numbers 4–6.

Number of Students at Highview School

Grade Level	Number of Students
Kindergarten	🧍🧍🧍🧍🧍🧍🧍🧍🧍
1st Grade	🧍🧍🧍🧍🧍🧍🧍🧍🧍🧍🧍🧍
2nd Grade	🧍🧍🧍🧍🧍🧍
3rd Grade	🧍🧍🧍🧍🧍🧍🧍🧍
4th Grade	🧍🧍🧍🧍🧍🧍🧍🧍🧍🧍🧍🧍
5th Grade	🧍🧍🧍🧍🧍🧍🧍

Key: 🧍 = 5 students

4. **How many students attend Highview School?**

   (F) 270 students

   (G) 290 students

   (H) 315 students

   (J) 192 students

5. **How many Highview students are fourth graders?**

   (A) 30 students

   (B) 40 students

   (C) 50 students

   (D) 60 students

6. **There are the same number of students in first grade and _____ grade.**

   (F) second

   (G) third

   (H) fourth

   (J) fifth

STOP

Name _____ Date _____

M4D1

Comparing Different Representations of Data

DIRECTIONS: The same data can be represented different ways depending on which style of chart is used. Use the information in the following table to fill in the bar graph and circle chart below.

School Election Results				
Grade	Votes for Blue Party	Votes for Red Party	Total Votes by Grade	Percentage of Total Votes
Third	25	5	30	33%
Fourth	10	16	26	28%
Fifth	15	21	36	39%
Total Votes by Party	50	42		

1.   **School Election Results**   **2.**   **Voters in Each Grade**

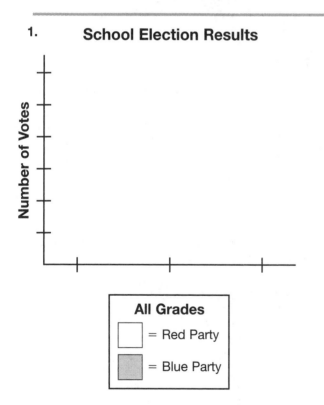

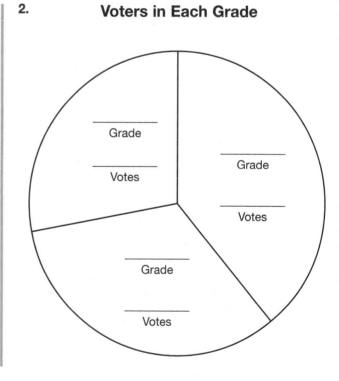

3. How well does the bar graph represent the data? The circle graph?

_____

_____

_____

Name _____ Date _____

Mathematics

| M4D1 |

For pages 105–106

Mini-Test 5

DIRECTIONS: Use the graph below for numbers 1–3.

Favorite Vacation Destination

Beach	🕶 🕶 🕶 🕶
Water Park	🕶 🕶 🕶 🕶 🕶
Amusement Park	🕶 🕶 🕶 🕶 🕶 🕶

Key: 🕶 = 8 votes

1. For how many votes does one symbol stand?

- Ⓐ   2 votes
- Ⓑ   5 votes
- Ⓒ   6 votes
- Ⓓ   8 votes

2. How many people answered this survey?

- Ⓕ $14\frac{1}{2}$ people
- Ⓖ   72 people
- Ⓗ   148 people
- Ⓙ   116 people

3. How many more people would rather go to an amusement park than the beach?

- Ⓐ   10 people
- Ⓑ   12 people
- Ⓒ   20 people
- Ⓓ   22 people

DIRECTIONS: The graph below shows the cost of a ticket to the movies in five different cities. Use the graph for numbers 4–6.

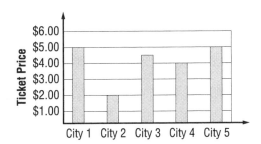

4. Which city has the cheapest movie tickets?

- Ⓕ   City 5
- Ⓖ   City 4
- Ⓗ   City 2
- Ⓙ   City 1

5. Which ticket price is found in more than one city?

- Ⓐ $4.00
- Ⓑ $10.00
- Ⓒ $2.00
- Ⓓ $5.00

6. How much more does it cost to buy a movie ticket in City 1 than in City 2?

- Ⓕ $5.00
- Ⓖ $3.00
- Ⓗ $2.00
- Ⓙ $4.00

STOP

Process Skills Standards

M4P. Process Skills

Students will apply mathematical concepts and skills in the context of authentic problems and will understand concepts rather than merely follow a sequence of procedures. Students will use the process standards as a way of acquiring and using content knowledge.

M4P1. Using the appropriate technology, students will solve problems that arise in mathematics and in other contexts. *(See pages 109–111.)*

a. Solve nonroutine word problems using the strategies of work backwards, use or make a table, and make an organized list as well as all strategies learned in previous grades.

b. Solve single- and multi-step routine word problems related to all appropriate fourth-grade math standards.

c. Determine the operation(s) needed to solve a problem.

d. Determine the most efficient way to solve a problem (mental math, paper/pencil, or calculator).

M4P2. Students will investigate, develop, and evaluate mathematical arguments. *(See page 112.)*

M4P3. Students will use the language of mathematics to express ideas precisely. *(See pages 113.)*

M4P4. Students will understand how mathematical ideas interconnect and build on one another and apply mathematics in other content areas. *(See page 114.)*

M4P5. Students will create and use pictures, manipulatives, models, and symbols to organize, record, and communicate mathematical ideas. *(See page 115.)*

Mathematics

M4P1

Using Strategies to Solve Problems

DIRECTIONS: Read and work each problem. Choose the best answer.

Example:

A store has 3,802 compact discs on the shelves. The store receives 2 new cases of compact discs. There are 320 compact discs in each case. How many compact discs does the store have now?

- (A) 640 compact discs
- (B) 3,802 compact discs
- (C) 4,442 compact discs
- (D) 3,482 compact discs

Answer: (C)

Clue

Work backwards, make a table, or make a list to help you solve some of the problems.

1. Grant went to get a frozen yogurt from the concession stand. He could choose vanilla, chocolate, or twist yogurt. He could have a cup, wafer cone, or sugar cone. How many possible combinations does Grant have?

- (A) 6 combinations
- (B) 3 combinations
- (C) 8 combinations
- (D) 9 combinations

2. How many more tickets were sold on Friday than on Tuesday?

CENTER CINEMAS
MOVIE TICKET SALES

MONDAY
TUESDAY
WEDNESDAY
THURSDAY
FRIDAY

KEY: 10 TICKETS =

- (F) 45 tickets
- (G) 55 tickets
- (H) 75 tickets
- (J) 295 tickets

3. If you wanted to compare the features of two different solid shapes, the best thing to use would be a _____ .

- (A) Venn diagram
- (B) pie chart
- (C) tally chart
- (D) line graph

4. Larry, Carey, and Harry went out for lunch. Each friend ordered a salad. The choices were egg, tuna, and chicken. Carey won't eat egg. Larry never orders tuna. Harry only likes chicken. Each friend ate something different. Who ordered tuna?

- (F) Larry
- (G) Carey
- (H) Harry
- (J) not enough information

GO

Name _____   Date _____

DIRECTIONS: Use the information below to help you solve questions 5–7.

You have a bag of candy to share with your class. There are 25 students in your class. You want each student to get 7 pieces.

5. **What operation will you need to use to figure out how many candies you need?**

   (A)   addition

   (B)   subtraction

   (C)   multiplication

   (D)   division

6. **How many candies do you need in all?**

   (F)   200 candies

   (G)   175 candies

   (H)   1,500 candies

   (J)   145 candies

7. **Two students are absent on the day you hand out the candies. Write a number sentence to show how many candies you will have left over.**

_____

_____

DIRECTIONS: Read and work each problem. Find the correct answer.

8. **A worker at Command Software makes $720 a week. You want to figure out how much he makes an hour. What other piece of information do you need?**

   (A)   the number of weeks the worker works each year

   (B)   the number of vacation days the worker takes

   (C)   how much money the worker makes each day

   (D)   how many hours a week the worker works

9. **You have coins that total $1.23. What coins do you have?**

   (F)   10 dimes, 1 nickel, 3 pennies

   (G)   3 quarters, 3 dimes, 3 pennies

   (H)   4 quarters, 1 dime, 2 nickels, 3 pennies

   (J)   4 quarters, 3 dimes, 3 pennies

DIRECTIONS: Jimmy wants to buy baseball cards for his collection. At a sale, the cards are being sold in packs. Look at the chart below. Use it to answer questions 10–12.

Number of Packs	Number of Cards
2	16
4	32
6	___
7	56

10. **What number sentence do you need to find the number of cards in each package?**

   (A) $2 \times 16 = $ ▉

   (B) $16 - 2 = $ ▉

   (C) $16 \div 2 = $ ▉

   (D) $56 - 7 = $ ▉

11. **What is the missing number in the chart?**

   (F)   38

   (G)   42

   (H)   48

   (J)   not enough information

12. **If Jimmy bought 3 packs of baseball cards, how many cards would he have altogether?**

   (A)   18 cards

   (B)   24 cards

   (C)   32 cards

   (D)   36 cards

STOP

Mathematics   **Process Skills**

M4P1

Determining
Number Operations

DIRECTIONS: Choose the best answer.

1. **What would be a fast way to add the same number 10 times?**
   - (A) Subtract 10 from the number.
   - (B) Divide the number by 10.
   - (C) Multiply the number by 10.
   - (D) Add 10 to the number.

2. **Hiking shoes usually cost $49. This week they are on sale for $7 less than the regular price. What is the sale price of hiking shoes?**
   - (F) $49 \times $7 = ▣
   - (G) $49 + $7 = ▣
   - (H) $49 - $7 = ▣
   - (J) $49 \div $7 = ▣

3. **There are 12 eggs in a dozen. Which number sentence shows how many eggs are in 3 dozen?**
   - (A) 12 \div 3 = ▣
   - (B) 12 - 3 = ▣
   - (C) 12 + 3 = ▣
   - (D) 12 \times 3 = ▣

4. **Suppose you had 15 objects and you wanted to put them into 5 boxes. How would you find out the number of objects that would fit into each box?**
   - (F) Divide 15 by 5.
   - (G) Multiply 15 by 5.
   - (H) Add 15 and 5.
   - (J) Subtract 5 from 15.

DIRECTIONS: Choose the correct operation to solve each problem.

5. **Steve brought 6 apples to the Math Club as a snack. If Steve and 3 members share the apples equally, how much does each person get?**
   - (A) addition
   - (B) subtraction
   - (C) multiplication
   - (D) division

6. **Mrs. Davidson is putting a fence around her garden. The garden has four sides, and each has a different length. What is the perimeter of Mrs. Davidson's garden?**
   - (F) addition
   - (G) subtraction
   - (H) multiplication
   - (J) division

7. **The sum of two numbers is 496. One number is 299. How do you find the other number?**
   - (A) addition
   - (B) subtraction
   - (C) multiplication
   - (D) division

8. **A number minus 20 equals 46. How do you find the number?**
   - (F) addition
   - (G) subtraction
   - (H) multiplication
   - (J) division

STOP

Mathematics

M4P2

Evaluating Mathematical Arguments

DIRECTIONS: Choose the best answer.

Clue — Before you choose an answer, ask yourself, "Does this answer make sense?"

1. **Which of the following would you probably measure in feet?**

   (A) length of a pencil

   (B) distance between two cities

   (C) amount of juice left in a bottle

   (D) the length of a couch

2. **You are mailing in your brother's college application today. It is a regular letter size. You must make sure you have enough postage. How much do you think it weighs?**

   (F) 1 pound   (H) 1 ounce

   (G) 8 pounds   (J) 8 ounces

3. **A yard is surrounded by 400 yards of fence. It took Lynne 8 days to paint the fence. Which number sentence can Lynne use to figure out how much fence she painted in a day?**

   (A) $400 \times 8 = \blacksquare$

   (B) $400 \div 8 = \blacksquare$

   (C) $400 - 8 = \blacksquare$

   (D) $400 + 8 = \blacksquare$

4. **Five students want to find their average height in inches. Their heights are 54 inches, 56 inches, 52 inches, 57 inches, and 53 inches. How would you find the average height of the students?**

   (F) Add the heights and multiply by 5.

   (G) Add the heights and divide by 5.

   (H) Add the heights and divide by the number of inches in 1 foot.

   (J) Multiply the heights and divide by the number of inches in 1 foot.

5. **Mr. Cook was 25 years old when Mary was born. How old will he be when Mary has her thirteenth birthday?**

   (A) 38 years old

   (B) 12 years old

   (C) 25 years old

   (D) 13 years old

6. **Write a number sentence to verify your answer to question 5.**

   _____

   _____

   _____

7. **Marcos has $47.82. He plans to spend $25 on presents. How much money will he have left, to the nearest dollar?**

   (F) $22

   (G) $22.82

   (H) $23

   (J) $25

8. **Write a number sentence to verify the answer to question 7.**

   _____

   _____

   _____

STOP

Mathematics   Process Skills

M4P3

Using Mathematical Language

DIRECTIONS: Describe how to solve each problem in the space provided.

1. If you burn 318 calories in 60 minutes of playing tennis, how many calories would you burn in 30 minutes? _____

4. A roller coaster holds a total of 184 people. If each car holds 8 people, how many cars are there? _____

2. A chicken pot pie was cut into 8 slices. For dinner, the Wilsons ate $\frac{3}{8}$ of the pie. For lunch, the Wilsons ate $\frac{1}{4}$ of the pie. How much of the pie was eaten? _____

5. Jesse bought a pack of cards for $1.25 and a baseball for $8.39. He has $5.36 left over. How much money did he start with? _____

3. There were 488 balloons decorating the gymnasium for a party. There were 97 students at the party. If each student brought home an equal number of balloons after the party, how many balloons were left over? _____

6. A box of 20 tennis balls costs $35.80. What is the cost for each tennis ball? _____

STOP

Mathematics

M4P4

Process Skills

Applying Math to Other Areas

DIRECTIONS: Choose the best answer.

1. The school basketball team has scored a total of 369 points during 9 games so far this season. What was the average number of points scored per game?

   (A) 47 points

   (B) 360 points

   (C) 40 points

   (D) 41 points

2. Garth took $15.00 to the art supply store. He spent $12.76 on art supplies. He wants to buy one more item that costs $2.50. Does he have enough money?

   (F) yes

   (G) no

3. A dripping faucet leaks 3.5 gallons of water each day. If the faucet leaks for 20 days before it is fixed, and the price of water is $0.30 per gallon, how much did the leak cost?

   (A) $10.50

   (B) $2.10

   (C) $21.00

   (D) $24.50

4. A company can produce 7,500 tons of ore per day. It takes 1 day to deliver the ore to customers. A customer wants 50,000 tons delivered in 9 days. It will pay a bonus if the ore can be delivered in 8 days. Can the company accept this job and will it receive a bonus?

   (F) cannot accept job

   (G) can accept job but will not receive a bonus

   (H) can accept job and will receive a bonus

   (J) cannot be determined

5. After a storm, it took 30 hours for the snow to melt. This is _____ .

   (A) the same as a week

   (B) about two days

   (C) between one and two days

   (D) the same as a day

6. Rita left dance class at 3:30 P.M. She arrived home at 4:17 P.M. How long did it take Rita to get home?

   (F) 1 hour, 17 minutes

   (G) 47 minutes

   (H) 37 minutes

   (J) 13 minutes

7. Look at the sign below. If you just missed the 2:10 show, how many minutes will you need to wait for the next one?

   (A) 50 minutes

   (B) 45 minutes

   (C) 60 minutes

   (D) 55 minutes

AMAZING DOLPHIN SHOW!

Daily at

1:15

2:10

3:05

4:00

4:50

Name _____   Date _____

M4P5

Using Pictures
to Solve Problems

DIRECTIONS: Choose the best answer.

1. Rayna wants to buy a toy that costs $1.39.
   She has the coins below. How much more
   does she need?

   Ⓐ $1.04
   Ⓑ 69¢
   Ⓒ 70¢
   Ⓓ $1.05

2. Which shape is missing from this pattern?

     ?

   Ⓕ   Ⓗ

   Ⓖ   Ⓙ

3. Which of the following sets of figures

   shows $\frac{1}{3}$ shaded?

   Ⓐ

   Ⓑ

   Ⓒ

   Ⓓ

4. In the picture below, 1 book stands for 5
   books. How many books does this picture
   stand for?

   Ⓕ 25
   Ⓖ 45
   Ⓗ 40
   Ⓙ 30

5. Kim made one straight cut across the
   trapezoid as shown. Which pair of figures
   could be the two cut pieces of the trapezoid?

   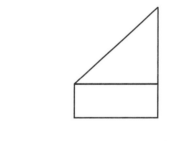

   Ⓐ

   Ⓑ

   Ⓒ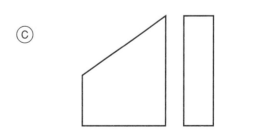

   Ⓓ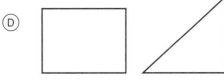

   STOP

115

Mathematics

M4P1–M4P5

For pages 109–115

Mini-Test 6

DIRECTIONS: Choose the best answer.

1. **Gerald's desk has 5 pencils, 3 erasers, and 2 boxes of crayons. There are 16 crayons in each box. How many crayons does Gerald have?**

   Ⓐ 30 crayons

   Ⓑ 10 crayons

   Ⓒ 26 crayons

   Ⓓ 32 crayons

2. **Which number sentence would you use to verify your answer to question 1?**

   Ⓕ 5 + 3 + 2

   Ⓖ 16 × 2

   Ⓗ 5 × 3 × 2

   Ⓙ 16 ÷ 2

3. **Each day 7,500 tons of ore can be processed. How many tons of ore can be processed in 25 days?**

   Ⓐ 188 tons

   Ⓑ 187,500 tons

   Ⓒ 188,000 tons

   Ⓓ 8 tons

4. **David scored 1,832 points on a video game. Susan scored 2 times more than David. Paul scored 234 points less than Susan. What was Paul's score?**

   Ⓕ 3,320 points

   Ⓖ 3,664 points

   Ⓗ 3,430 points

   Ⓙ 468 points

5. **Which process would you use to determine Paul's score?**

   Ⓐ Multiply David's score by 2.

   Ⓑ Multiply David's score by 2 and add 234.

   Ⓒ Multiply David's score by 2 and subtract 234.

   Ⓓ Multiply 234 by 2 and add David's score.

6. **An auto dealer hopes to sell twice as many cars this year as last year. He sold 1,056 cars last year. What operation will you need to use to figure out how many cars the dealer hopes to sell this year?**

   Ⓕ addition

   Ⓖ subtraction

   Ⓗ multiplication

   Ⓙ division

7. **How did the temperature change between Saturday and Sunday? On Sunday it was _____ .**

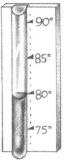 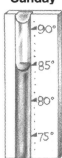

| Saturday | Sunday |

   Ⓐ 5 degrees cooler than Saturday

   Ⓑ 10 degrees cooler than Saturday

   Ⓒ 5 degrees warmer than Saturday

   Ⓓ 10 degrees warmer than Saturday

116

How Am I Doing?

Mini-Test 1

Pages 83–84

Number Correct

18–22 answers correct	**Great Job!** Move on to the section test on page 119.
12–17 answers correct	**You're almost there!** But you still need a little practice. Review practice pages 69–82 before moving on to the section test on page 119.
0–11 answers correct	**Oops!** Time to review what you have learned and try again. Review the practice section on pages 69–82. Then retake the test on pages 83–84. Now move on to the section test on page 119.

Mini-Test 2

Page 90

Number Correct

7 answers correct	**Awesome!** Move on to the section test on page 119.
4–6 answers correct	**You're almost there!** But you still need a little practice. Review practice pages 86–89 before moving on to the section test on page 119.
0–3 answers correct	**Oops!** Time to review what you have learned and try again. Review the practice section on pages 86–89. Then retake the test on page 90. Now move on to the section test on page 119.

Mini-Test 3

Page 99

Number Correct

8 answers correct	**Great Job!** Move on to the section test on page 119.
4–7 answers correct	**You're almost there!** But you still need a little practice. Review practice pages 92–98 before moving on to the section test on page 119.
0–3 answers correct	**Oops!** Time to review what you have learned and try again. Review the practice section on pages 92–98. Then retake the test on page 99. Now move on to the section test on page 119.

How Am I Doing?

Mini-Test 4

Page 103

Number Correct

8–9 answers correct	**Great Job!** Move on to the section test on page 119.
4–7 answers correct	**You're almost there!** But you still need a little practice. Review practice pages 101–102 before moving on to the section test on page 119.
0–3 answers correct	**Oops!** Time to review what you have learned and try again. Review the practice section on pages 101–102. Then retake the test on page 103. Now move on to the section test on page 119.

Mini-Test 5

Page 107

Number Correct

6 answers correct	**Awesome!** Move on to the section test on page 119.
4–5 answers correct	**You're almost there!** But you still need a little practice. Review practice pages 105–106 before moving on to the section test on page 119.
0–3 answers correct	**Oops!** Time to review what you have learned and try again. Review the practice section on pages 105–106. Then retake the test on page 107. Now move on to the section test on page 119.

Mini-Test 6

Page 116

Number Correct

7 answers correct	**Great Job!** Move on to the section test on page 119.
4–6 answers correct	**You're almost there!** But you still need a little practice. Review practice pages 112–115 before moving on to the section test on page 119.
0–3 answers correct	**Oops!** Time to review what you have learned and try again. Review the practice section on pages 112–115. Then retake the test on page 116. Now move on to the section test on page 119.

Name _____ Date _____

Final Mathematics Test
for pages 69–116

DIRECTIONS: Choose the best answer.

1. **What is the word name for 46,703,405?**

   (A) forty six million, seven zero three thousand, four hundred five

   (B) forty six million, seven hundred three thousand, four hundred fifty

   (C) forty six million, seven hundred three thousand, four hundred five

   (D) forty six million, seven hundred three, four hundred five

2. **What is 3,080 rounded to the nearest hundred?**

   (F) 3,100

   (G) 3,000

   (H) 3,070

   (J) 3,090

3. **What is 1.36 rounded to the nearest whole number?**

   (A) 2.0

   (B) 1.0

   (C) 1.4

   (D) 1.3

4. **Find 7.31 − 0.52.**

   (F) 6.79

   (G) 7.83

   (H) 7.21

   (J) 6.21

5. **Find 81 ÷ 9.**

   (A) 6

   (B) 7

   (C) 8

   (D) 9

6. **Find 354 × 73.**

   (F) 25,842

   (G) 2,478

   (H) 1,062

   (J) 427

7. **Find 77)847.**

   (A) 25

   (B) 11

   (C) 14

   (D) 21

8. **Which decimal below names the smallest number?**

   (F) 0.06

   (G) 0.6

   (H) 0.64

   (J) 6.40

9. **Which of these is the same as $\frac{3}{10}$ of a pizza?**

   (A) 0.35

   (B) 0.60

   (C) 0.30

   (D) 0.40

10. **Add the missing number to make the fraction equivalent. $\frac{1}{4} = \frac{\blacksquare}{8}$**

    (F) 1

    (G) 2

    (H) 3

    (J) 4

GO →

Name _____ Date _____

DIRECTIONS: Choose the correct answer for numbers 11–12. Remember to reduce fraction answers to simplest form. Choose "none of the above" if the correct answer is not given.

11. Find $4\frac{6}{11} + 3\frac{2}{11}$.

    (A)   8

    (B) $1\frac{4}{11}$

    (C) $7\frac{8}{11}$

    (D)   none of the above

12. Find $\frac{18}{15} - \frac{9}{15}$.

    (F) $\frac{28}{15}$

    (G) $\frac{13}{15}$

    (H) $\frac{3}{5}$

    (J)   none of the above

DIRECTIONS: Choose the best answer.

13. Find $(6 \times 4) - 10$.

    (A)   24

    (B)   14

    (C)   46

    (D)   0

14. Find $15 \div (5 - 2)$.

    (F)   5

    (G)   1

    (H)   2.5

    (J)   15

15. Find $(5 + 2) \times (4 + 3)$.

    (A)   31

    (B)   16

    (C)   49

    (D)   120

16. Which of the following expressions is equal to $6 + 7 + 3$?

    (F) $6 + 7 - 3$

    (G) $6 \times 7 + 3$

    (H) $3 + 7 \times 6$

    (J) $3 + 7 + 6$

17. Which of the following expressions is equal to the expression $4(3 + 7)$?

    (A) $(4 \times 3) + 7$

    (B) $4 + 10$

    (C) $3 + (4 \times 7)$

    (D) $(4 \times 3) + (4 \times 7)$

18. Mr. Werner bought a 5-pound roast beef. How many ounces did the roast beef weigh?

    (F)   8 ounces

    (G)   80 ounces

    (H)   10 ounces

    (J)   50 ounces

19. The load limit on a small bridge is 8 tons. What is the load limit in pounds?

    (A)   16,000 pounds

    (B)   1,600 pounds

    (C)   160 pounds

    (D)   8,000 pounds

20. 16 kilograms is how many grams?

    (F)   16 grams

    (G)   160 grams

    (H)   1,600 grams

    (J)   16,000 grams

21. What is the degree measure of the angle made when the minute hand on a clock travels from 3:20 to 3:50?

    (A)   90°

    (B)   180°

    (C)   270°

    (D)   360°

GO

Name _____   Date _____

22. What type of angle is shown?

- (F) right
- (G) acute
- (H) obtuse
- (J) none of these

23. These lines are _____ .

- (A) parallel
- (B) perpendicular
- (C) none of these

24. What type of triangle is shown?

- (F) acute
- (G) right
- (H) obtuse
- (J) none of these

25. How many faces does a cube have?

- (A) 3
- (B) 4
- (C) 5
- (D) 6

26. How many sides does a trapezoid have?

- (F) 5
- (G) 4
- (H) 3
- (J) 2

DIRECTIONS: Use the graph below for questions 27–28.

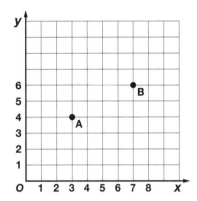

27. What are the coordinates for point A?

- (A) (7, 6)
- (B) (4, 3)
- (C) (7, 4)
- (D) (3, 4)

28. What are the coordinates for point B?

- (F) (7, 6)
- (G) (4, 3)
- (H) (6, 7)
- (J) (7, 4)

DIRECTIONS: Choose the best answer.

29. Find the missing number.

18, 26, 22, _____ , 26, 34, 30, 38

- (A) 24
- (B) 28
- (C) 30
- (D) 32

30. Extend the number pattern.

56, 53, 55, 52, 54, 51, 53, _____

- (F) 50
- (G) 55
- (H) 49
- (J) 51

GO

DIRECTIONS: For numbers 31–32, let $y = 19 - 2x$.

31. **What is y when x is 3?**
    - (A) 25
    - (B) 13
    - (C) 17
    - (D) 10

32. **What is y when x is 5?**
    - (F) 9
    - (G) 17
    - (H) 24
    - (J) 26

33. **Jill bought 5 books. Each book cost $3.95. Which number sentence shows how much she paid for all 5 books?**
    - (A) $5 + \$3.95 = $ ▨
    - (B) $5 \times \$3.95 = $ ▨
    - (C) $5 - \$3.95 = $ ▨
    - (D) $\$3.95 + \$3.95 = $ ▨

34. **Which number can you put in the ▨ to make the number sentence true?**

    $$10 - 6 < \text{▨}$$
    - (F) 2
    - (G) 3
    - (H) 4
    - (J) 5

35. **What makes this number sentence true?**
    $67 - $ ▨ $= 26$
    - (A) 93
    - (B) 41
    - (C) 67
    - (D) 26

36. **What makes this number sentence true?**
    ▨ $\times 20 = 640$
    - (F) 620
    - (G) 660
    - (H) 12,800
    - (J) 32

DIRECTIONS: Use the bar graph below to answer questions 37–39. The following information is based on the different kinds of sandwiches sold at a sandwich shop in one week.

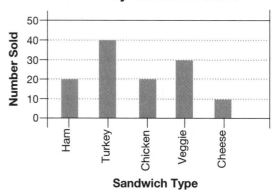

Weekly Sandwich Sales

37. **How many ham sandwiches were sold during the week?**
    - (A) 30 ham sandwiches
    - (B) 20 ham sandwiches
    - (C) 10 ham sandwiches
    - (D) 40 ham sandwiches

38. **How many sandwiches were sold altogether?**
    - (F) 120 sandwiches
    - (G) 12 sandwiches
    - (H) 100 sandwiches
    - (J) 40 sandwiches

39. **Which kind of sandwich was sold the most?**
    - (A) Chicken
    - (B) Turkey
    - (C) Veggie
    - (D) Cheese

GO

40. There are 32 girls in a relay race. Four run on each team. Which number sentence shows how to find the number of teams there are?

- (F) $32 + 4 = $ ▧
- (G) $32 - 4 = $ ▧
- (H) $32 \times 4 = $ ▧
- (J) $32 \div 4 = $ ▧

41. A tank contains 555 liters of oil. Nine liters of oil are used each day. Approximately how many days will the supply last?

- (A) 40 days
- (B) 50 days
- (C) 60 days
- (D) 70 days

42. Which number is missing from this table?

4	7
9	12
15	▧

- (F) 13
- (G) 14
- (H) 15
- (J) 18

43. Noriko was looking at a map of Glacier National Park. He noted the heights of five mountain peaks: Rockwell at 9,272 feet; Going-to-the-Sun at 9,642 feet; Thunderbird at 8,520 feet; Kaina at 9,489 feet; and Cleveland at 10,466 feet. If the mountains were arranged in order of height, which mountain would be in the middle?

- (A) Kaina
- (B) Going-to-the-Sun
- (C) Thunderbird
- (D) Rockwell

44. Alex's fourth-grade class was having its class party. There are 120 fourth graders, but 5 were absent that day. How many students attended the class party?

- (F) 115 students
- (G) 125 students
- (H) 24 students
- (J) 105 students

45. Toby left his house for school at 7:35 A.M. He arrived at school at 7:50 A.M., which was 10 minutes before school started. How long before school started did Toby leave the house?

- (A) 10 minutes
- (B) 15 minutes
- (C) 25 minutes
- (D) not enough information

STOP

Name _____   Date _____

Final Mathematics Test
Answer Sheet

1 (A) (B) (C) (D)   21 (A) (B) (C) (D)
2 (F) (G) (H) (J)   22 (F) (G) (H) (J)
3 (A) (B) (C) (D)   23 (A) (B) (C)
4 (F) (G) (H) (J)   24 (F) (G) (H) (J)
5 (A) (B) (C) (D)   25 (A) (B) (C) (D)
6 (F) (G) (H) (J)   26 (F) (G) (H) (J)
7 (A) (B) (C) (D)   27 (A) (B) (C) (D)
8 (F) (G) (H) (J)   28 (F) (G) (H) (J)
9 (A) (B) (C) (D)   29 (A) (B) (C) (D)
10 (F) (G) (H) (J)   30 (F) (G) (H) (J)

11 (A) (B) (C) (D)   31 (A) (B) (C) (D)
12 (F) (G) (H) (J)   32 (F) (G) (H) (J)
13 (A) (B) (C) (D)   33 (A) (B) (C) (D)
14 (F) (G) (H) (J)   34 (F) (G) (H) (J)
15 (A) (B) (C) (D)   35 (A) (B) (C) (D)
16 (F) (G) (H) (J)   36 (F) (G) (H) (J)
17 (A) (B) (C) (D)   37 (A) (B) (C) (D)
18 (F) (G) (H) (J)   38 (F) (G) (H) (J)
19 (A) (B) (C) (D)   39 (A) (B) (C) (D)
20 (F) (G) (H) (J)   40 (F) (G) (H) (J)

                         41 (A) (B) (C) (D)
                         42 (F) (G) (H) (J)
                         43 (A) (B) (C) (D)
                         44 (F) (G) (H) (J)
                         45 (A) (B) (C) (D)

Georgia Social Studies
Content Standards

The social studies section measures knowledge in four different areas:

1) History

2) Geography

3) Government/Civics

4) Economics

Georgia Social Studies
Table of Contents

History Standards

SS4H1. The student will describe how early Native-American cultures developed in North America. *(See page 128.)*
a. Locate where the American Indians settled with emphasis on Arctic (Inuit), Northwest (Kwakiutl), Plateau (Nez Perce), Southwest (Hopi), Plains (Pawnee), and Southeastern (Seminole).
b. Describe how the American Indians used their environment to obtain food, clothing, and shelter.

SS4H2. The student will describe European exploration in North America. *(See page 129.)*
a. Describe the reasons for, obstacles to, and accomplishments of the Spanish, French, and English explorations of John Cabot, Vasco Nunez de Balboa, Juan Ponce de Leon, Christopher Columbus, Henry Hudson, and Jacques Cartier.
b. Describe examples of cooperation and conflict between Europeans and Native Americans.

SS4H3. The student will explain the factors that shaped British colonial America. *(See page 130.)*
a. Compare and contrast life in the New England, Mid-Atlantic, and Southern colonies.
b. Describe colonial life in America as experienced by various people, including large landowners, farmers, artisans, women, indentured servants, slaves, and Native Americans.

SS4H4. The student will explain the causes, events, and results of the American Revolution. *(See page 131.)*
a. Trace the events that shaped the revolutionary movement in America, including the French and Indian War, British Imperial Policy that led to the 1765 Stamp Act, the slogan "no taxation without representation," the activities of the Sons of Liberty, and the Boston Tea Party.
b. Explain the writing of the Declaration of Independence, including who wrote it, how it was written, why it was necessary, and how it was a response to tyranny and the abuse of power.
c. Describe the major events of the Revolution and explain the factors leading to American victory and British defeat, including the Battles of Lexington and Concord, and Yorktown.
d. Describe key individuals in the American Revolution with emphasis on King George III, George Washington, Benjamin Franklin, Thomas Jefferson, Benedict Arnold, Patrick Henry, and John Adams.

SS4H5. The student will analyze the challenges faced by the new nation. *(See page 132.)*
a. Identify the weaknesses of the government established by the Articles of Confederation.
b. Identify the major leaders of the Constitutional Convention (James Madison and Benjamin Franklin) and describe the major issues they debated: the rights of states, the Great Compromise, slavery.
c. Identify the three branches of the U.S. government as outlined by the Constitution, describe what they do, how they relate to each other (checks and balances and separation of powers), and how they relate to the states.

History Standards

d. Identify and explain the rights in the Bill of Rights, describe how the Bill of Rights places limits on the power of government, and explain the reasons for its inclusion in the Constitution in 1791.
e. Describe the causes of the War of 1812, including burning of the Capitol and the White House.

SS4H6. The student will explain westward expansion of America between 1801 and 1861. *(See page 133.)*
a. Describe territorial expansion with emphasis on the Louisiana Purchase, the Lewis & Clark expedition, and the acquisitions of Texas (the Alamo and independence), Oregon (Oregon Trail), and California (Gold Rush and the development of mining towns).
b. Describe the impact of the steamboat, the steam locomotive, and the telegraph on life in America.

SS4H7. The student will examine the main ideas of the abolitionist and suffrage movements. *(See page 134.)*
a. Discuss biographies of Harriet Tubman and Elizabeth Cady Stanton.
b. Explain the significance of Sojourner Truth's Address ("Ain't I a Woman?" 1851) to the Ohio Women's Rights Convention.

Name _____ Date _____

SS4H1   Impact of the Environment on Native Americans

DIRECTIONS: Different Native-American cultures lived in different environments. Read about some of them below. Then answer the questions.

Native Americans of the Eastern Forests: This environment had plenty of rain. The summers were especially warm and rainy. It had large, lush forests and many lakes and streams that were home to abundant fish and game. They planted corn, pumpkin, squash, beans, tobacco, and gourds. They did not need to search for wild food.

Native Americans of the Plains: This environment had rolling, grassy prairie lands but few trees. The trees grew mainly beside rivers. Large herds of animals such as elk, deer, antelope, and buffalo grazed on the prairie. The tribes followed the herds across the plains.

Native Americans of the Southwest: This environment was high and dry. Most of the rain fell in the summer when it could help plants grow. Winter snow from the mountains supplied water for streams, springs, and water holes. The Pueblos developed irrigation and were able to grow their food.

Native Americans of the Desert: The Seed Gatherers lived in the driest parts of California and other western desert regions. There were few game animals. They gathered berries, nuts, seeds, and roots for food. They ground the seeds into flour for gruel.

Native Americans of the Northwest: This environment had heavy rainfall along the northern Pacific coast. The ocean and the rivers were full of fish. It had tall, dense forests. They gathered bulbs, berries, and seeds.

Native Americans of the Far North: This environment was frozen under ice and snow for at least half of the year. Most vegetables would not grow here, and there were very few trees.

1. **Which of the following do you think was the main source of food for Native Americans of the Far North?**

   Ⓐ snow and ice

   Ⓑ cows, pigs, and chickens

   Ⓒ fish and Arctic sea and land animals

   Ⓓ wheat and fruit

2. **Native Americans of the Desert were less likely to grow their own food because**

   _____ .

   Ⓕ they lived in the driest parts of California

   Ⓖ they did not like to farm

   Ⓗ they did not like to search for food

   Ⓙ they had plenty of game animals to hunt

3. **Which of the following do you think were least likely to be expert fishers?**

   Ⓐ Native Americans of the Northwest

   Ⓑ Native Americans of the Desert

   Ⓒ Native Americans of the Far North

   Ⓓ Native Americans of the Eastern Forests

4. **Native Americans of the Eastern Forests did not gather much of their food. Why not?**

   Ⓕ Other Native American societies brought food to them.

   Ⓖ They were lazy.

   Ⓗ Their environment was harsh and most vegetable foods did not flourish there.

   Ⓙ They knew how to grow their own food.

Name _____   Date _____

Social Studies   **History**

SS4H2   # European Exploration

DIRECTIONS: Choose the best answer.

1. Which of the following explorers attempted unsuccessfully to discover a northern trade route between Europe and Asia?
   - (A) Vasco Nunez de Balboa
   - (B) Henry Hudson
   - (C) Jacques Cartier
   - (D) Juan Ponce de Leon

2. Which of the following explorers was the first European to sight the Pacific Ocean?
   - (F) John Cabot
   - (G) Christopher Columbus
   - (H) Juan Ponce de Leon
   - (J) Vasco Nunez de Balboa

3. Which of the following explorers led the first expedition up the St. Lawrence River?
   - (A) Juan Ponce de Leon
   - (B) Jacques Cartier
   - (C) John Cabot
   - (D) Henry Hudson

4. Which of the following explorers made the first English voyage to North America?
   - (F) Henry Hudson
   - (G) Christopher Columbus
   - (H) Jacques Cartier
   - (J) John Cabot

5. Which of the following explorers led the first expedition to reach what is now Florida?
   - (A) Christopher Columbus
   - (B) Vasco Nunez de Balboa
   - (C) Juan Ponce de Leon
   - (D) John Cabot

6. Which of the following explorers was the first to sail west across the Atlantic Ocean in search of a sea route to Asia?
   - (F) Christopher Columbus
   - (G) John Cabot
   - (H) Vasco Nunez de Balboa
   - (J) Juan Ponce de Leon

7. France based its claims to territory in what is now Canada on the explorations of which of the following people?
   - (A) Juan Ponce de Leon
   - (B) John Cabot
   - (C) Jacques Cartier
   - (D) Henry Hudson

8. Which of the following explorers was one of the first to claim part of the North American mainland for Spain?
   - (F) John Cabot
   - (G) Juan Ponce de Leon
   - (H) Christopher Columbus
   - (J) Jacques Cartier

9. Which of the following explorers gave England a claim to the mainland of North America and led to the founding of English colonies in America?
   - (A) Christopher Columbus
   - (B) Jacques Cartier
   - (C) Juan Ponce de Leon
   - (D) John Cabot

Social Studies

| SS4H3 |

Colonial Life

DIRECTIONS: Choose the best answer.

1. **Which of the following groups of people generally produced soap for the use of the family and sometimes for sale?**

    (A) indentured servants

    (B) women

    (C) artisans

    (D) slaves

2. **In which of the colonies was tobacco an important crop?**

    (F) New England

    (G) Mid-Atlantic

    (H) Southern

    (J) none of the above

3. **Rural life was most common in which of the colonies?**

    (A) Mid-Atlantic

    (B) Southern

    (C) New England

    (D) Rural life was equally spread throughout the colonies.

4. **Houses in colonial America were most often made of which material?**

    (F) brick

    (G) wood

    (H) mud

    (J) thatch

5. **You own an eight-room, two-story house in a colony. You are most likely a(n) _____ .**

    (A) merchant

    (B) artisan

    (C) small farmer

    (D) large landowner

DIRECTIONS: Read the passage and then answer the questions.

During colonial times, indentured slaves and servants were a main part of the work force. Both groups often worked as farm laborers, although they could also be crafts workers.

Indentured servants had a contract, or legal agreement, that specified the amount of time they would work for their masters. Once they had met the terms of the contract, they achieved their freedom. They could grow crops, such as tobacco, or serve a role in government.

Slaves, on the other hand, had few rights and could be bought and sold from one master to another. They were expected to grow large quantities of crops but could not make any money doing so.

6. **Which of the following groups most often worked in the fields?**

    (F) artisans

    (G) slaves

    (H) Native Americans

    (J) women

7. **Based on the passage, which of the following statements is true?**

    (A) Indentured servants enjoyed more rights than slaves.

    (B) Slaves made contracts with their masters.

    (C) Slaves enjoyed more rights than indentured servants.

    (D) Neither slaves nor servants worked on farms.

STOP

Name _____   Date _____

Social Studies   **History**

Causes of the American Revolution

DIRECTIONS: Read the passage. Then answer the questions.

> In the mid-1700s, Great Britain defeated France in the French and Indian War. As a result, it won vast new lands in North America. Unfortunately, the war was very expensive. Great Britain tried to make up some of the money it spent fighting the war by taxing the colonists.
>
> Though the tax angered colonists, the way Great Britain created the tax angered them even more. Normally, the assembly elected by a colony decided the money matters for that colony. But this time, no assembly had been allowed to help decide. The British Parliament made this decision. Angry assembly members said the tax was unfair since they had no hand in it. The British took back this tax, but later passed another tax. This angered the colonists even more. They became outraged when British soldiers shot several protesting colonists in what was named the Boston Massacre. Many colonists began to fear the British soldiers. They considered them to be the enemy.

1. **One way the French and Indian War contributed to American independence was that _____ .**

   (A) it cost Great Britain a lot of money, which it tried to make up by taxing the colonists

   (B) all traces of French influence were removed from North America

   (C) British soldiers left North America and the colonists took control

   (D) all of the above

2. **Which of the following was *not* a major cause of the American Revolution?**

   (F) Colonists were feeling much more independent because the French were no longer in North America.

   (G) Great Britain tried to ban all but one religion in the colonies.

   (H) Colonists feared the British soldiers in North America might turn against them.

   (J) Many colonists resented being taxed by the British without having any representation in the British Parliament.

3. **What happened when the colonists protested the taxing by the British?**

   (A) The British Parliament decided to remove the tax.

   (B) The French and Indian War started.

   (C) The British decided to tax the colonies even more.

   (D) British soldiers shot several of the protestors.

4. **Which of the following men played an important role as a soldier during the American Revolution and also became the first president of the United States?**

   (F) Andrew Jackson

   (G) Abraham Lincoln

   (H) George Washington

   (J) Samuel Adams

Social Studies

SS4H5

Early Government

DIRECTIONS: Choose the best answer.

1. **How many states had to approve an amendment to the Articles of Confederation?**
   - (A) a simple majority
   - (B) all of them
   - (C) two thirds
   - (D) three fourths

2. **Which of the following statements is true?**
   - (F) Under the Articles of Confederation, Congress had the power to levy taxes.
   - (G) The Articles of Confederation provided for a strong central government.
   - (H) Under the Articles of Confederation, states each had one vote in Congress.
   - (J) Under the Articles of Confederation, Congress had the power to regulate trade.

3. **Which leader of the Constitutional Convention is known as the "Father of the Constitution"?**
   - (A) James Wilson
   - (B) Benjamin Franklin
   - (C) Roger Sherman
   - (D) James Madison

4. **According to the _____ Plan, a state's population would determine the number of representatives it had in the legislature.**
   - (F) Virginia
   - (G) New Jersey
   - (H) Connecticut
   - (J) Georgia

5. **The Great Compromise proposed that states would have equal representation in _____ .**
   - (A) Congress
   - (B) the House of Representatives
   - (C) the Senate
   - (D) the Supreme Court

6. **Which branch of government established by the Constitution is responsible for implementing and enforcing laws?**
   - (F) legislative
   - (G) executive
   - (H) federalist
   - (J) judicial

7. **The system where each branch of government has the ability to limit the power of the other branches is known as _____ .**
   - (A) checks and balances
   - (B) separation of powers
   - (C) limitation of powers
   - (D) branch monitoring

8. **The first ten amendments of the Constitution are known as the Bill of Rights. Which of the amendments states that any powers not given to the national government and not denied to the states belong to the states or the people?**
   - (F) First
   - (G) Fourth
   - (H) Ninth
   - (J) Tenth

Westward Expansion

DIRECTIONS: Choose the best answer.

1. The Louisiana Purchase covered lands between the _____ and the _____ and doubled the territory of the United States.

   (A) Mississippi River, Rocky Mountains

   (B) Mississippi River, Pacific Ocean

   (C) Appalachian Mountains, Mississippi River

   (D) Appalachian Mountains, Pacific Ocean

2. The Lewis and Clark expedition gave the United States a claim to what territory?

   (F) Missouri

   (G) Louisiana

   (H) Oregon

   (J) Texas

3. The Republic of Texas achieved independence and voted in favor of annexation to the United States in 1836. In what year was it admitted to the Union?

   (A) 1836

   (B) 1837

   (C) 1845

   (D) 1846

4. The route used by many pioneers to travel to the Pacific Northwest, crossing 2,000 miles with a beginning point in Independence, Missouri, is known as the _____ .

   (F) Santa Fe Trail

   (G) Oregon Trail

   (H) California Trail

   (J) Mormon Trail

5. What led to the population growth that allowed California to apply for statehood?

   (A) Reports of the mild climate led to the arrival of thousands of pioneers.

   (B) Many immigrants in search of a new life were arriving by ship.

   (C) The discovery of gold by James Marshall led to the Gold Rush.

   (D) New railroad lines brought people to the area.

DIRECTIONS: Read the passage and then answer the question.

The inventions of the steamboat and steam locomotive changed transportation in America. They made it easier to move people and goods across the country. Steamboats traveled on the waterways, and locomotives traveled on the railroads that soon linked all parts of the United States. As a result, the travel time from one destination to another decreased dramatically. If certain goods were not available in their location, people could have them delivered more quickly and cheaply than ever before. They could also send goods or crops they had produced to other areas of the country.

6. Which of the following describes the impact of these two inventions on transportation in America?

   (F) They had no impact on transportation.

   (G) They only had a minor impact on transportation.

   (H) They had a significant impact on transportation.

   (J) There is not enough information.

STOP

Social Studies   **History**

SS4H7

Abolitionist and Suffrage Movements

DIRECTIONS: Read the passage and then answer the questions.

During their lifetimes, Harriet Tubman and Elizabeth Cady Stanton both worked to improve the rights of Americans. Tubman was closely associated with the abolitionist movement, or the movement to end slavery, and Stanton was involved with the women's suffrage movement, or the movement to help women gain the right to vote.

Harriet Tubman is most well known for her role as a "conductor" of the Underground Railroad. Tubman was born as a slave in Maryland and worked as both a house servant and field hand. She later married a free African American named John Tubman. Five years after her marriage, she feared she would be sold and decided to run away from the plantation where she lived. She safely made her way to Pennsylvania and soon found work. Soon, however, she returned to Maryland to help free her sister and her sister's children. This was the first of 19 dangerous trips she would make to the South over a period of 10 years. As a conductor, she led over 300 slaves to freedom.

In 1848, Elizabeth Cady Stanton attended an antislavery convention. When women were not officially recognized at the convention, Stanton helped launch the suffrage movement by organizing the first women's rights convention, which was held in Seneca Falls, New York. She also worked with Susan B. Anthony and founded the National Woman Suffrage Association. She spoke out for the suffrage cause. She was an editor of *The Revolution,* which was a weekly women's suffrage paper. Stanton died in 1902, 20 years before women were granted the right to vote in the United States.

1. **What was the goal of the abolitionist movement?**

   _____

   _____

   _____

2. **Which of the following statements about Harriet Tubman is *not* true?**

   Ⓐ She was a conductor of the Underground Railroad.

   Ⓑ She married a slave named John Tubman.

   Ⓒ She helped free her sister from slavery.

   Ⓓ She made 19 trips to the South to help free slaves.

3. **What was the goal of the women's suffrage movement?**

   _____

   _____

   _____

4. **Which of the following statements about Elizabeth Cady Stanton is *not* true?**

   Ⓕ She was an editor of a women's suffrage paper.

   Ⓖ She attended an antislavery convention.

   Ⓗ She helped found a women's rights association.

   Ⓙ She lived to see women gain the right to vote in the United States.

Social Studies

| SS4H1–SS4H7 |

History

Mini-Test 1

For pages 128–134

DIRECTIONS: Choose the best answer.

1. **Which of the following Native-American settlements would you most likely have found in present-day Arizona?**

   (A) Native Americans of the Eastern Forests

   (B) Native Americans of the Far North

   (C) Native Americans of the Northwest

   (D) Native Americans of the Southwest

2. **Which of the following Native-American groups often hunted buffalo for food?**

   (F) Native Americans of the Southwest

   (G) Native Americans of the Plains

   (H) Native Americans of the Northwest

   (J) Native Americans of the Far North

3. **Which of the following explorers was from France?**

   (A) Henry Hudson

   (B) Christopher Columbus

   (C) Jacques Cartier

   (D) John Cabot

4. **Which explorer gave the Pacific Ocean its name?**

   (F) Ponce de Leon

   (G) Vasco Nunez do Balboa

   (H) Jacques Cartier

   (J) Christopher Columbus

5. **Which of the following had contracts, or legal agreements, with their masters?**

   (A) merchants

   (B) slaves

   (C) artisans

   (D) indentured servants

6. **Colonists protested taxation by the British because _____ .**

   (F) British soldiers had shot colonists during the Boston Massacre

   (G) they felt they should only be taxed by their own representatives

   (H) they did not like the British

   (J) they wanted independence from Britain

7. **Which of the following proposed that states have equal representation in the Senate?**

   (A) the Virginia Plan

   (B) the Articles of Confederation

   (C) the Great Compromise

   (D) the Bill of Rights

8. **How many amendments of the Constitution make up the Bill of Rights?**

   (F) four

   (G) seven

   (H) ten

   (J) twelve

9. **The United States purchased Louisiana from _____ .**

   (A) Spain

   (B) France

   (C) Great Britain

   (D) Mexico

STOP

Geography Standards

SS4G1. The student will be able to locate important physical and man-made features in the United States. *(See page 137.)*

a. Locate major physical features of the United States, including the Atlantic Coastal Plain, Great Plains, Continental Divide, Great Basin, Death Valley, Gulf of Mexico, St. Lawrence River, and the Great Lakes.

b. Locate major man-made features, including New York City, New York; Boston, Massachusetts; Philadelphia, Pennsylvania; and the Erie Canal.

SS4G2. The student will describe how physical systems affect human systems. *(See page 138.)*

a. Explain why each of the Native-American groups (SS4H1.a) occupied the areas they did, with emphasis on why some developed permanent villages and others did not.

b. Describe how the early explorers (SS4H2.a) adapted, or failed to adapt, to the various physical environments in which they traveled.

c. Explain how the physical geography of each colony helped determine economic activities practiced therein.

d. Explain how each force (Americans and British) attempted to use the physical geography of each battle site to their benefit (SS4H4.c).

e. Describe physical barriers that hindered and physical gateways that benefited territorial expansion from 1801 to 1861 (SS4H6.a).

Social Studies

| SS4G1 |

Locating Features

DIRECTIONS: Match the descriptions in Column A with the features in Column B.

COLUMN A

1. _____ a continuous ridge that runs along the top of the Rocky Mountains and separates the flow of water between the Pacific and Atlantic Oceans

2. _____ the lowest, hottest, driest region in the United States that is located in east-central California and parts of Nevada

3. _____ bodies of water that surround the state of Michigan

4. _____ a low plateau that runs between the eastern United States and the Appalachian Mountains

5. _____ an historic waterway located in New York State that connects Lake Erie with the Hudson River

6. _____ a desert region that covers most of Nevada and parts of California, Idaho, Utah, Wyoming, and Oregon

7. _____ a waterway that runs between Lake Ontario and the Atlantic Ocean

8. _____ a region of grasslands, hills, valleys, and streams that stretches eastward from the Rocky Mountains to South Dakota, Nebraska, Kansas, and Oklahoma

9. _____ a body of water that borders Florida, Alabama, Mississippi, Louisiana, and Texas

COLUMN B

a. Atlantic Coastal Plain

b. Continental Divide

c. Death Valley

d. Erie Canal

e. Great Basin

f. Great Lakes

g. Great Plains

h. Gulf of Mexico

i. St. Lawrence River

Social Studies   Geography

Impact of Geography

DIRECTIONS: Choose the best answer.

1. **Which of the following best explains why Native Americans of the Plains were less likely to settle into permanent villages?**

   (A) Their main food source was always on the move.

   (B) They did not like to farm.

   (C) They did not like to eat vegetables and fruits.

   (D) They were unable to build their own dwellings.

2. **Farming to obtain food requires time. This leads people to develop permanent villages. Which of the following Native-American groups developed settlements due to their farming practices?**

   (F) Native Americans of the Desert

   (G) Native Americans of the Far North

   (H) Native Americans of the Eastern Forests

   (J) Native Americans of the Northwest

3. **Fertile soil, large coastal plains, and a favorable climate caused which of the following colonies to engage in large-scale farming as an economic activity?**

   (A) New England

   (B) Mid-Atlantic

   (C) Southern

   (D) both A and B

4. **Which of the following colonies engaged in whaling, lumber, and fur-trading activities as a result of its geographic location?**

   (F) Southern

   (G) New England

   (H) Mid-Atlantic

   (J) both F and H

5. **During the Revolutionary War, British troops were waiting for supplies to be delivered to them by way of the York River. The troops took up a defensive position at Yorktown while they waited. What was one way the American forces used the area's geography to defeat the British forces in the Battle of Yorktown?**

   (A) They waited until the supplies came down the river and then attacked the British from behind.

   (B) Naval forces created a blockade at Chesapeake Bay. This prevented the British ships from delivering supplies to the troops and prevented the British troops from using the river as a way of escape.

   (C) They built a dam across the York River to prevent the British from using the river to escape.

   (D) none of the above

6. **What was the major physical barrier to U.S. expansion to the Pacific Northwest?**

   (F) Mississippi River

   (G) Great Plains

   (H) Appalachian Mountains

   (J) Rocky Mountains

STOP

Social Studies

SS4G1–SS4G2

Mini-Test 2

For pages 137–138

DIRECTIONS: Choose the best answer.

1. **Which of the following is a large desert region located in the western United States?**
   - (A) Gulf of Mexico
   - (B) Great Plains
   - (C) Continental Divide
   - (D) Great Basin

2. **The St. Lawrence River _____ .**
   - (F) links Lake Erie and the Hudson River
   - (G) forms part of the border between the state of New York and the province of Ontario, Canada
   - (H) flows east to west
   - (J) divides the flow of water between the Pacific and Atlantic Oceans

3. **Which of the following borders the southeastern coast of the United States?**
   - (A) Great Lakes
   - (B) Gulf of Mexico
   - (C) Erie Canal
   - (D) Death Valley

4. **Which of the following is a vast dry grassland stretching across the central part of the United States?**
   - (F) Atlantic Coastal Plain
   - (G) Continental Divide
   - (H) Great Plains
   - (J) Death Valley

5. **Which of the following is located in California?**
   - (A) Gulf of Mexico
   - (B) Death Valley
   - (C) St. Lawrence River
   - (D) Continental Divide

8. **Which of the following forms part of the boundary between the United States and Canada?**
   - (F) Atlantic Coastal Plain
   - (G) Great Plains
   - (H) Great Lakes
   - (J) Erie Canal

7. **The Continental Divide _____ .**
   - (A) stretches from Cape Cod through the southeast United States and through Mexico
   - (B) runs along the top of the Rocky Mountains from Canada to Mexico
   - (C) divides the United States in two equal halves, west and east
   - (D) divides the United States into two equal halves, north and south

8. **Which of the following explains why Native Americans of the Northwest were most likely expert fishers?**
   - (F) The region had heavy rainfall.
   - (G) They did not like to hunt for game.
   - (H) The region was covered with tall, dense forests.
   - (J) The oceans and rivers were full of fish.

STOP

Government/Civics Standards

SS4CG1. The student will describe the meaning of: *(See page 141.)*
a. natural rights as found in the Declaration of Independence (the right to life, liberty, and the pursuit of happiness).
b. "We the people" from the Preamble to the U.S. Constitution as reflecting consent of the governed, or popular sovereignty.
c. the federal system of government in the United States.

SS4CG2. The student will explain the importance of freedom of expression as explained in the First Amendment to the U.S. Constitution. *(See page 142.)*

SS4CG3. The student will describe the functions of government. *(See page 143.)*
a. Explain the process for making and enforcing laws.
b. Explain managing conflicts and protecting rights.
c. Describe providing for the defense of the nation.
d. Explain limiting the power of people in authority.
e. Explain the fiscal responsibility of government.

SS4CG4. The student will explain the importance for Americans to share certain central democratic beliefs and principles, both personal and civic. *(See page 144.)*
a. Explain the necessity of respecting the rights of others and promoting the common good.
b. Explain the necessity of obeying reasonable laws/rules voluntarily, and explain why it is important for citizens in a democratic society to participate in public (civic) life (staying informed, voting, volunteering, communicating with public officials).

SS4CG5. The student will name positive character traits of key historic figures and government leaders (honesty, patriotism, courage, trustworthiness). *(See page 145.)*

SS4CG1

Natural Rights

DIRECTIONS: Read the passage, and then complete the activity that follows.

Declaration of Independence

In 1776, the American colonists declared their independence from Great Britain in the Declaration of Independence. The document is made up of four parts. The first part is the preamble, or introduction. It explains the reasons why the colonists wanted to form a new country. The second part tells what the Americans believed were rights that all people have. The third part lists the complaints against the British King George III. The fourth part declares the colonies' independence from Britain.

The second part of the Declaration of Independence contains the following words: "We hold these truths to be self-evident, that all men are created equal, that they are endowed by their Creator with certain unalienable Rights, that among these are Life, Liberty, and the pursuit of Happiness."

 Unalienable rights are rights that cannot be taken away.

The quotation above refers to three rights—the right to life, liberty (or freedom), and the pursuit of happiness. Write a paragraph describing how these rights still apply to the lives of Americans today.

_____

_____

_____

_____

_____

_____

_____

_____

_____

_____

_____

_____

STOP

Social Studies

SS4CG2

Freedom of Expression

DIRECTIONS: Read the passage, and then answer the questions.

First Amendment Rights

The First Amendment of the U.S. Constitution protects the civil liberties of individuals in the United States. It states: "Congress shall make no law respecting an establishment of religion, or prohibiting [forbidding] the free exercise thereof; or abridging the freedom of speech, or of the press; or the right of the people peaceably to assemble, and to petition the Government for a redress of grievances."

This amendment grants Americans the freedom of religion, or the right to practice any religion they choose. The other three freedoms are called "freedoms of expression." The freedom of speech and the press allow people to speak or write without the government interfering. The freedom of assembly allows people to gather together for peaceful and lawful purposes. And the freedom to petition guarantees people the right to ask the government to provide relief for a wrong through the courts or other governmental action.

1. **Why is it important for people in a democracy to be able to practice these freedoms?**

_____
_____
_____
_____
_____
_____
_____
_____
_____
_____
_____
_____
_____

2. **Imagine that a new amendment was approved that took away one of these freedoms. How would that affect the way you live? What things would you no longer be able to do without this freedom?**

_____
_____
_____
_____
_____
_____
_____
_____
_____
_____
_____

STOP

Social Studies   Government/Civics

SS4CG3

Making and Enforcing Laws

DIRECTIONS: Choose the best answer.

1. **The legislative branch of government is responsible for _____ .**
   - (A) making laws
   - (B) enforcing laws
   - (C) interpreting laws
   - (D) all of the above

2. **A draft of a proposed law is called a(n) _____ .**
   - (F) junior law
   - (G) bill
   - (H) issue
   - (J) veto

3. **A bill may be introduced in the _____ .**
   - (A) House of Representatives
   - (B) Supreme Court
   - (C) Senate
   - (D) either A or C

4. **What happens after Congress passes a bill?**
   - (F) It becomes law.
   - (G) It is sent to the president to sign.
   - (H) It is put on a ballot for voters to approve.
   - (J) It is passed on to the Supreme Court for approval.

5. **The president may choose to reject a bill. The term given for this action is _____ .**
   - (A) annexation
   - (B) approval
   - (C) veto
   - (D) prohibition

6. **Proposed laws, or legislation, is evaluated by _____ .**
   - (F) each member of Congress
   - (G) committees of selected members of Congress
   - (H) members of the Supreme Court
   - (J) the Chief Justice of the Supreme Court

7. **What percentage of the House and Senate must vote in favor of a bill to override a presidential veto?**
   - (A) three fourths
   - (B) two thirds
   - (C) just over one half
   - (D) The vote must be unanimous.

8. **Which branch of the government is responsible for enforcing laws?**
   - (F) judicial
   - (G) legislative
   - (H) executive
   - (J) all of the above

STOP

Social Studies   Government/Civics

SS4CG4 # Rights and Responsibilities
of Citizens

DIRECTIONS: Choose the best answer.

1. **Every right has a responsibility that goes with it. For example, as Americans, we have the right to free speech. But this right means that we must also be sure _____ .**

   (A) never to criticize the government

   (B) to write to the president at least once every year

   (C) that the things we say are accurate and truthful

   (D) to silence any viewpoint we disagree with

2. **To be a responsible citizen, all Americans should _____ .**

   (F) obey the law

   (G) stay informed about current events

   (H) vote

   (J) all of the above

3. **In the United States, every citizen over the age of 18 has the right to vote. What are some responsibilities citizens have when it comes to voting? Explain your answer.**

   _____

   _____

   _____

   _____

   _____

   _____

   _____

   _____

DIRECTIONS: Read the passage and then answer the question.

   William was a U.S. citizen. William, however, did not like many things the president and Congress were doing. He thought their actions were wrong and immoral. So, William used his computer to make a booklet that told how much he disliked the U.S. government. He printed many copies of the booklet. Then, he went downtown and gave the booklets to people he passed on the street. If someone did not want the booklet, William simply moved on to the next person.

   Jane did not like what William wrote in the booklet. She asked a police officer, who was patrolling nearby, to stop William from passing out his booklets.

4. **Did William and Jane respect the rights of others? Why or why not?**

   _____

   _____

   _____

   _____

   _____

   _____

   _____

   _____

   _____

   _____

   _____

   _____

   _____

STOP

Social Studies   **Government/Civics**

SS4CG5

Identifying
Character Traits

DIRECTIONS: Choose a historic figure or government leader that you admire. Write a short essay describing how this person modeled positive character traits, such as honesty, patriotism, courage, or trustworthiness. For example, George Washington showed courage in battle when facing the enemy. He showed patriotism in fighting for and later leading the United States as its first president. He also modeled trustworthiness when he surrendered his power at the end of the Revolutionary War and refused to become a monarch-type, or king-like, leader.

_____

_____

_____

_____

_____

_____

_____

_____

_____

_____

_____

_____

_____

_____

_____

_____

_____

_____

_____

_____

_____

_____

_____

STOP

Social Studies

Government/Civics

SS4CG1–SS4CG5

Mini-Test 3

For pages 141–145

DIRECTIONS: Choose the best answer.

1. **The right to life, liberty, and the pursuit of happiness is given to the American people in which U.S. document?**
   - (A) Articles of Confederation
   - (B) Declaration of Independence
   - (C) U.S. Constitution
   - (D) Gettysburg Address

2. **In the Preamble to the Constitution, "We the People of the United States" reflects what concept of government?**
   - (F) popular sovereignty, or rule by the people
   - (G) checks and balances
   - (H) federalism
   - (J) separation of powers

3. **Freedom of speech, press, assembly, and petition are known as our rights to freedom of _____ .**
   - (A) religion
   - (B) nature
   - (C) expression
   - (D) participation

4. **Which amendment to the U.S. Constitution guarantees the rights described in question 3?**
   - (F) Third
   - (G) First
   - (H) Fifth
   - (J) Second

5. **Who can veto a bill that was passed by Congress?**
   - (A) the Chief Justice of the Supreme Court
   - (B) the vice president of the United States
   - (C) the president of the United States
   - (D) all of the above

6. **Which level of government is responsible for making laws?**
   - (F) judicial
   - (G) legislative
   - (H) executive
   - (J) all levels can make laws

7. **A law passed by a state applies to _____ .**
   - (A) all U.S. citizens
   - (B) the citizens of that state
   - (C) no one—laws cannot be passed by state governments
   - (D) none of the above

8. **Which of the following is *not* an acceptable way of participating in public life?**
   - (F) joining a peaceful protest march
   - (G) boycotting a company's products if you oppose their practices
   - (H) starting a riot in which property and people's lives are damaged in order to make sure your views receive media coverage
   - (J) writing a letter to the newspaper editor expressing your opinion on a tax increase

Economics Standards

SS4E1. The student will use the basic economic concepts of *trade, opportunity cost, specialization, voluntary exchange, productivity,* and *price incentives* to illustrate historical events. *(See page 148.)*

a. Describe *opportunity costs* and their relationship to decision-making across time (such as decisions to send expeditions to the New World).

b. Explain how *price incentives* affect people's behavior and choices (such as colonial decisions about what crops to grow and products to produce).

c. Describe how *specialization* improves standards of living (such as how specific economies in the three colonial regions developed).

d. Explain how voluntary exchange helps both buyers and sellers (such as prehistoric and colonial trade in North America).

e. Describe how *trade* promotes economic activity (such as trade activities in the early nation were managed differently under the Articles of Confederation and the Constitution).

f. Give examples of technological advancements and their impact on business *productivity* during the development of the United States.

SS4E2. The student will identify the elements of a *personal budget* and explain why personal *spending* and *saving* decisions are important. *(See page 149.)*

Economic Effects

DIRECTIONS: Choose the best answer.

1. **You are trying to decide between purchasing a game and a video. You only have enough money to buy one of these items. You finally decide to purchase the video and give up the game. In this scenario, the game was your _____ , the next best alternative you give up when you make a choice.**

   Ⓐ specialization

   Ⓑ trade

   Ⓒ opportunity cost

   Ⓓ expense

2. **Which of the following would have been an opportunity cost to Spain of *not* sending an expedition to the New World?**

   Ⓕ They would have had funds available for another purpose.

   Ⓖ They would not have been able to expand their territory overseas.

   Ⓗ They would have had more ships available in case of naval warfare.

   Ⓙ none of the above

3. **Which of the following reasons best explains why people in the Southern colonies grew tobacco?**

   Ⓐ The colonists were unable to grow any other crops.

   Ⓑ Tobacco was easy to grow.

   Ⓒ The colonists enjoyed growing it for personal use.

   Ⓓ The demand for tobacco in Europe was greater than the supply, which kept the price of it high.

4. **How did the invention of the electric lightbulb help businesses become more productive?**

   Ⓕ Business could operate more easily at night.

   Ⓖ It led to an increase in the number of factories.

   Ⓗ It allowed people to specialize in their tasks.

   Ⓙ all of the above

DIRECTIONS: Read the following situation, and then answer the question that follows.

You are a pioneer family living in a new area west of the Mississippi River. Your nearest neighbors are the Yorks, who live 10 miles away. You both live about 50 miles away from the nearest town. Your family and the Yorks have been producing your own food and clothing.

Both families soon realize that each family has some special skills and resources that the other family does not have. Your family is good at farming and is able to grow more corn that the Yorks. The Yorks, on the other hand, are able to hunt more animals for meat.

5. **In what way would the families be better off if each family specialized in only one area and traded with the other?**

   _____

   _____

   _____

   _____

   _____

   _____

Name _____ Date _____

SS4E2   **Personal Budget**

DIRECTIONS: Choose the best answer.

1. A financial plan that helps people make the best possible use of their money is a(n) _____ .

   (A) savings account
   (B) income
   (C) budget
   (D) expense

2. The amount of money you earn or receive during a certain period of time is referred to as your _____ .

   (F) savings
   (G) expenses
   (H) outflow
   (J) income

3. In a budget, the items that you spend money on are referred to as _____ .

   (A) expenses
   (B) income
   (C) savings
   (D) products

4. Since you have only a certain amount of money to spend, you should _____ .

   (F) buy everything that you want
   (G) decide which expenses are the most important and put money aside to pay for those items
   (H) pay for expenses from least to most expensive, regardless of priority
   (J) choose the most expensive item you can afford and buy it

5. Which of the following is *not* a potential expense you might include in a budget?

   (A) food
   (B) allowance
   (C) clothes
   (D) computer games

6. Which of the following outcomes should cause you to rethink your budget?

   (F) Your income equals your expenses.
   (G) Your expenses are less than your income.
   (H) Your expenses are greater than your income.
   (J) Your income is greater than your expenses.

7. A *need* is something you must have for survival, such as food and water. A *want* is something you would like to have, but it is not necessary. Which of these items is it most important to include in a budget?

   (A) needs only
   (B) wants only
   (C) They should be budgeted for equally.
   (D) cannot tell from this information

8. Why is it important to save money? Explain your answer.

   _____
   _____
   _____
   _____

STOP

149

Social Studies

Economics

SS4E1–SS4E2

Mini-Test 4

For pages 148–149

DIRECTIONS: Read the following passage and then answer questions 1–3.

> After the Revolutionary War, British merchants flooded the United States with inexpensive British goods. This caused many American artisans and merchants to go out of business because they could not compete with the low prices of the British goods. To fight back, states placed taxes upon or restricted British imports, but these taxes were different from one state to the next. As a result, some of the states had lower taxes on imported goods than other states. The British tried to have their goods imported by the states with the lowest taxes or fewest restrictions. Once their goods were in the states, they attempted to move them into the other states that had tried to keep them out.
>
> Since the Confederate Congress was not allowed to regulate or control trade, the states began setting up posts on their borders to prevent the British from taking advantage of the different trade laws. They also began levying taxes on goods coming from other states in order to raise the profits in their own state. In this sense, each state acted as its own country.

1. When a tax is levied or placed upon goods, how does it affect the price of those goods?

(A) It lowers the price of the goods.

(B) The price of the goods stays the same.

(C) It raises the price of the goods.

(D) none of the above

2. How did American workers try to protect their economic interests after the Revolutionary War?

(F) They raised the prices on their goods.

(G) The lowered the prices on their goods.

(H) They levied taxes on or restricted British imports.

(J) all of the above

3. How did the British try to take advantage of the states' attempt to restrict British imports?

(A) They stopped exporting goods to the United States.

(B) They exported their goods to the states with the lowest taxes.

(C) They exported their goods to the states with the highest taxes.

(D) They levied taxes on American imports.

DIRECTIONS: Choose the best answer.

4. Your income is _____ .

(F) the items you spend money on

(G) the amount of money you earn during a certain period of time

(H) the money you save for certain items

(J) something you would like to have but do not necessarily need

STOP

How Am I Doing?

Mini-Test 1	8–9 answers correct	**Great Job!** Move on to the section test on page 153.
Page 135 **Number Correct**	4–7 answers correct	**You're almost there!** But you still need a little practice. Review practice pages 128–134 before moving on to the section test on page 153.
	0–3 answers correct	**Oops!** Time to review what you have learned and try again. Review the practice section on pages 128–134. Then retake the test on page 135. Now move on to the section test on page 153.
Mini-Test 2	8 answers correct	**Awesome!** Move on to the section test on page 153.
Page 139 **Number Correct**	4–7 answers correct	**You're almost there!** But you still need a little practice. Review practice pages 137–138 before moving on to the section test on page 153.
	0–3 answers correct	**Oops!** Time to review what you have learned and try again. Review the practice section on pages 137–138. Then retake the test on page 139. Now move on to the section test on page 153.
Mini-Test 3	8 answers correct	**Great Job!** Move on to the section test on page 153.
Page 146 **Number Correct**	4–7 answers correct	**You're almost there!** But you still need a little practice. Review practice pages 141–145 before moving on to the section test on page 153.
	0–3 answers correct	**Oops!** Time to review what you have learned and try again. Review the practice section on pages 141–145. Then retake the test on page 146. Now move on to the section test on page 153.

How Am I Doing?

Mini-Test 4	4 answers correct	**Awesome!** Move on to the section test on page 153.
Page 150 **Number Correct**	3 answers correct	**You're almost there!** But you still need a little practice. Review practice pages 148–149 before moving on to the section test on page 153.
	0–2 answers correct	**Oops!** Time to review what you have learned and try again. Review the practice section on pages 148–149. Then retake the test on page 150. Now move on to the section test on page 153.

Name _____ Date _____

Final Social Studies Test
for pages 128–150

DIRECTIONS: Choose the best answer.

1. The Native Americans of the _____ lived in an environment with plenty of rain, lush forests, and many lakes and streams with abundant game and fish.
   - (A) Southwest
   - (B) Plains
   - (C) Eastern Forests
   - (D) Far North

2. How did the Native Americans in question 1 obtain their food?
   - (F) They planted crops.
   - (G) They hunted seals and caribou.
   - (H) They gathered fruits and berries.
   - (J) They hunted buffalo.

3. Which of the following explorers claimed the Pacific Ocean and all of its shores for Spain?
   - (A) Christopher Columbus
   - (B) John Cabot
   - (C) Juan Ponce de Leon
   - (D) Vasco Nunez de Balboa

4. Which of the following was an English explorer who was the first European to discover the mainland of North America?
   - (F) John Cabot ✕
   - (G) Christopher Columbus ✕
   - (H) Ponce de Leon ✓
   - (J) Jacques Cartier ✕

5. Shipbuilding became prevalent in which of the following colonies?
   - (A) Mid-Atlantic ✕
   - (B) New England ✓
   - (C) Southern ✕
   - (D) Shipbuilding was not practiced in colonial America. ✕

6. Why were there a greater number of slaves living in the Southern colonies?
   - (F) The climate there was similar to what they had experienced in Africa. ✕
   - (G) Growing tobacco required a great deal of care and labor, and slaves were the least expensive help farmers could get.
   - (H) Slavery was banned in the Mid-Atlantic and New England colonies.
   - (J) all of the above

7. Which of the following wars took place during the mid-1700s and resulted in Great Britain winning vast new lands in North America?
   - (A) French and Indian War ✓
   - (B) Civil War ✕
   - (C) Revolutionary War ✕
   - (D) War of 1812 ✕

8. The Great Compromise _____ .
   - (F) determined how slaves would be counted for representation ✕
   - (G) resulted in the Bill of Rights
   - (H) divided Congress into two houses
   - (J) all of the above

9. The Constitution established how many branches of government?
   - (A) two
   - (B) three
   - (C) four
   - (D) five

GO

10. **Which branch of government established by the Constitution is responsible for interpreting laws?**

   (F) executive
   (G) judicial
   (H) federalist
   (J) legislative

11. **No person serving in one branch of the government may serve in any other branch at the same time. This is an example of _____ .**

   (A) limited government
   (B) federalism
   (C) checks and balances
   (D) separation of powers

12. **The California Gold Rush most likely increased the population of which of the following places?**

   (F) New Orleans, Louisiana
   (G) Chicago, Illinois
   (H) San Francisco, California
   (J) San Antonio, Texas

13. **As a result of the Louisiana Purchase, the United States _____ in land size.**

   (A) doubled
   (B) tripled
   (C) grew 20 percent
   (D) grew 50 percent

14. **Which of the following people led slaves to safety via the Underground Railroad?**

   (F) Harriet Tubman
   (G) Elizabeth Cady Stanton
   (H) Sojourner Truth
   (J) Harriet Beecher Stowe

15. **Which of the following is located in the state of New York?**

   (A) Boston
   (B) Philadelphia
   (C) Erie Canal
   (D) Death Valley

16. **The Atlantic Coastal Plain is _____ .**

   (F) a vast natural grassland bordering the Atlantic Ocean
   (G) a low plateau that runs between the eastern United States and the Appalachian Mountains
   (H) primarily a desert area
   (J) a continuous ridge that runs along the top of the Rocky Mountains

17. **Which of the following has the Rocky Mountains as its western border and stretches east to South Dakota, Nebraska, Kansas, and Oklahoma?**

   (A) Continental Divide
   (B) Great Plains
   (C) Great Basin
   (D) Death Valley

18. **On which border of the United States will you find the Great Lakes?**

   (F) western
   (G) eastern
   (H) northern
   (J) southern

19. **Which of the following is not found in the eastern United States?**

   (A) Great Basin
   (B) Atlantic Coastal Plain
   (C) Erie Canal
   (D) St. Lawrence River

GO

20. Which of the following is located west of the Appalachian Mountains?

- (F) Continental Divide
- (G) Death Valley
- (H) Great Plains
- (J) all of the above

21. Which of the following borders Florida, Alabama, Mississippi, Louisiana, and Texas?

- (A) St. Lawrence River
- (B) Gulf of Mexico
- (C) Great Lakes
- (D) Erie Canal

22. The wooded, mountainous geography of the New England colonies did not lend itself to which of the following industries?

- (F) fur trading
- (G) manufacturing
- (H) large-scale farming
- (J) woodworking

23. Control of what important physical feature was gained in the Louisiana Purchase?

- (A) the Rocky Mountains
- (B) the Mississippi River
- (C) the Ohio River
- (D) the Erie Canal

24. Under the federal system of government, some powers _____ .

- (F) belong to the federal government
- (G) belong to the states
- (H) are shared by the states and the federal government
- (J) all of the above

25. Which of the following is *not* a freedom of expression granted in the First Amendment?

- (A) freedom of speech
- (B) freedom to bear arms
- (C) freedom of the press
- (D) freedom to peaceably assemble

26. As a citizen, you have a responsibility to take part in your community. Which of the following is *not* a good way to do this?

- (F) write to the president of a company protesting the treatment of women in the company's commercial
- (G) read the newspaper regularly
- (H) secretly remove books from the library that you think are unpatriotic
- (J) vote in every election

27. Rule by the people is the basis of the concept of _____ .

- (A) federalism
- (B) constitutionalism
- (C) governmentalism
- (D) popular sovereignty

28. Enforcement of laws is the responsibility of which branch of government?

- (F) executive
- (G) legislative
- (H) judicial
- (J) each branch has this responsibility

29. A bill must be passed by _____ before it is sent to the president to sign.

- (A) the Supreme Court
- (B) Congress
- (C) the House of Representatives
- (D) the Senate

GO

30. **As Americans, we have many rights. Every right, however, has a _____ that goes with it.**

(F) consequence

(G) test

(H) problem

(J) responsibility

31. **Paul Revere rode to warn the colonists of the advancing British armies. Which of the following traits does this illustrate?**

(A) trustworthiness

(B) honesty

(C) patriotism

(D) all of the above

32. **Which of the following inventions enabled businesses to be more productive because they could operate at night as well as during the day?**

(F) cotton gin

(G) electric lightbulb

(H) telegraph

(J) steam locomotive

33. **In the mid-1800s, much of the South remained agricultural rather than moving toward manufacturing. Many farmers relied on cotton as their main crop. Which of the following explains their reason for doing so?**

(A) Textile mills in Europe were expanding and demanding all the cotton they could get, which raised the prices they were willing to pay.

(B) Cotton was the only crop that would grow on their land.

(C) The price of cotton was falling, so farmers grew more in order to make what they had previously earned.

(D) Manufacturing offered the opportunity to earn greater wealth but cotton production was easier.

34. **Opportunity cost can best be described as _____ .**

(F) the price of one item over another

(G) what is lost if you do not take advantage of the situation

(H) the next best alternative you give up when you make a choice

(J) all of the above

35. **All of the following are considered needs except for _____ .**

(A) food

(B) shelter

(C) entertainment

(D) clothing

36. **Which of the following is a potential source of income you might use to help you plan your personal budget?**

(F) allowance

(G) babysitting money

(H) pay for mowing lawns

(J) all of the above

STOP

Name _____ Date _____

Final Social Studies Test
Answer Sheet

1. (A) (B) (C) (D)
2. (F) (G) (H) (J)
3. (A) (B) (C) (D)
4. (F) (G) (H) (J)
5. (A) (B) (C) (D)
6. (F) (G) (H) (J)
7. (A) (B) (C) (D)
8. (F) (G) (H) (J)
9. (A) (B) (C) (D)
10. (F) (G) (H) (J)

11. (A) (B) (C) (D)
12. (F) (G) (H) (J)
13. (A) (B) (C) (D)
14. (F) (G) (H) (J)
15. (A) (B) (C) (D)
16. (F) (G) (H) (J)
17. (A) (B) (C) (D)
18. (F) (G) (H) (J)
19. (A) (B) (C) (D)
20. (F) (G) (H) (J)

21. (A) (B) (C) (D)
22. (F) (G) (H) (J)
23. (A) (B) (C) (D)
24. (F) (G) (H) (J)
25. (A) (B) (C) (D)
26. (F) (G) (H) (J)
27. (A) (B) (C) (D)
28. (F) (G) (H) (J)
29. (A) (B) (C) (D)
30. (F) (G) (H) (J)

31. (A) (B) (C) (D)
32. (F) (G) (H) (J)
33. (A) (B) (C) (D)
34. (F) (G) (H) (J)
35. (A) (B) (C) (D)
36. (F) (G) (H) (J)

Georgia Science
Content Standards

The science section measures knowledge in five different areas:

1) **Characteristics of Science**
   a. Habits of Mind
   b. The Nature of Science

2) **Content**
   a. Earth Science
   b. Physical Science
   c. Life Science

Georgia Science
Table of Contents

Habits of Mind Standards

S4CS1. Students will be aware of the importance of curiosity, honesty, openness, and skepticism in science and will exhibit these traits in their own efforts to understand how the world works. *(See page 161.)*

a. Keep records of investigations and observations and do not alter the records later.
b. Carefully distinguish observations from ideas and speculation about those observations.
c. Offer reasons for findings and consider reasons suggested by others.
d. Take responsibility for understanding the importance of being safety conscious.

S4CS2. Students will have the computation and estimation skills necessary for analyzing data and following scientific explanations. *(See page 162.)*

a. Add, subtract, multiply, and divide whole numbers using mental math, paper/pencil, and a calculator.
b. Use fractions and decimals, and translate between decimals and commonly encountered fractions—halves, thirds, fourths, fifths, tenths, and hundredths (but not sixths, sevenths, and so on)—in scientific calculations.
c. Judge whether measurements and computations of quantities, such as length, area, volume, weight, or time, are reasonable answers to scientific problems by comparing them to typical values.

S4CS3. Students will use tools and instruments for observing, measuring, and manipulating objects in scientific activities utilizing safe laboratory procedures. *(See page 163.)*

a. Choose appropriate common materials for making simple mechanical constructions and repairing things.
b. Measure and mix dry and liquid materials in prescribed amounts, exercising reasonable safety.
c. Use computers, cameras, and recording devices for capturing information.
d. Identify and practice accepted safety procedures in manipulating science materials and equipment.

S4CS4. Students will use ideas of system, model, change, and scale in exploring scientific and technological matters. *(See page 164.)*

a. Observe and describe how parts influence one another in things with many parts.
b. Use geometric figures, number sequences, graphs, diagrams, sketches, number lines, maps, and stories to represent corresponding features of objects, events, and processes in the real world. Identify ways in which the representations do not match their original counterparts.
c. Identify patterns of change in things—such as steady, repetitive, or irregular change—using records, tables, or graphs of measurements where appropriate.

S4CS5. Students will communicate scientific ideas and activities clearly. *(See page 165.)*

a. Write instructions that others can follow in carrying out a scientific procedure.
b. Make sketches to aid in explaining scientific procedures or ideas.
c. Use numerical data in describing and comparing objects and events.
d. Locate scientific information in reference books, back issues of newspapers and magazines, CD-ROMs, and computer databases.

Habits of Mind Standards

S4CS6. Students will question scientific claims and arguments effectively.
(See page 166.)

a. Support statements with facts found in books, articles, and databases, and identify the sources used.

b. Identify when comparisons might not be fair because some conditions are different.

Science

| S4SC1 |

Science Practices

DIRECTIONS: Read about Jeannie's experiment and then answer the questions.

My Question: Is warm water more dense than cold water?

What I Already Know: If two objects take up the same amount of space, the lighter one will be less dense.

What I Did: I filled a beaker with 100 mL of cold water. Then I filled another beaker with 100 mL of hot water, and I used red food coloring to color it red. I used an eyedropper to put the warm, red water into the beaker of cold water.

What Happened: The drops of red water floated to the top of the beaker. The red water made a layer on top of the layer of cold water in the beaker.

1. **Jeannie can conclude from her experiment that _____ .**
   - (A) warm water is more dense than cold water
   - (B) warm water is less dense than cold water
   - (C) warm water and cold water have the same density
   - (D) neither warm nor cold water have any density

2. **What phenomenon does this experiment help Jeannie understand?**
   - (F) why it rains in the summer
   - (G) why cold water boils so slowly
   - (H) why the top layer of the ocean is warmer than the lower layers
   - (J) why it is hard to make sugar dissolve in iced tea

DIRECTIONS: Read about Adam's experiment and then answer the questions.

Adam wants to find out how lemon juice reacts when it is combined with different substances. In three separate paper cups, he puts equal amounts of baking soda, salt, and sugar. Then he puts three drops of lemon juice into each cup. After 30 seconds, he observes all three cups.

3. **What is the variable you observe in this experiment?**
   - (A) the lemon juice
   - (B) the amount of time that passed
   - (C) the size of the cup
   - (D) the type of substance in the cups

4. **What should Adam do if he wants his lab partner to be able to repeat this experiment?**
   - (F) Keep accurate records of procedures and results.
   - (G) Wait until he finishes all the trials before recording any results.
   - (H) Estimate the amounts of materials used.
   - (I) none of these

5. **What would you expect to happen if Adam repeated this experiment with the cups in ice?**
   - (A) any reaction would happen slower
   - (B) the cups would melt
   - (C) any reaction would happen faster
   - (D) nothing different

STOP

Name _____   Date _____

Science   **Habits of**
Mind
| S4SC2 |

Using Fractions and Decimals

DIRECTIONS: Choose the best answer.

1. You mix 200 mL of a solution for an experiment. You are then asked to transfer $\frac{3}{10}$ of this solution into another container. How much solution will you need to measure out into the second container?

   (A) 30 mL
   (B) 60 mL
   (C) 67 mL
   (D) 6 mL

2. How would you record $\frac{3}{10}$ in decimal notation?

   (F) 3.10
   (G) 0.03
   (H) 0.3
   (J) 0.003

3. You recorded the high temperature for the 30 days in June. During that time, $\frac{1}{5}$ of the days had temperatures of 90°F or above. How many days had highs of at least 90°F?

   (A) 6 days
   (B) 5 days
   (C) 15 days
   (D) 18 days

4. Using the data in question 3, how would you record in decimal form how many days in June had highs below 90°F?

   (F) 0.08
   (G) 4.5
   (H) 0.45
   (J) 0.8

5. Hansa is a four-year-old female Asian elephant. She currently weighs 3,450 pounds. If she weighed $\frac{7}{100}$ of this amount when she was born, which of the following is the closest estimate to her birth weight?

   (A) 240 pounds
   (B) 490 pounds
   (C) 200 pounds
   (D) 290 pounds

6. You planted 20 seeds for an experiment. Of these, 12 sprouted. What percentage of the seeds germinated?

   (F) 60%
   (G) $\frac{6}{10}$
   (H) 0.6
   (J) all of the above

7. You repeat the experiment and plant another 20 seeds. This time $\frac{2}{5}$ of the seeds sprout. How many seedlings grew from this batch?

   (A) 5 seedlings
   (B) 8 seedlings
   (C) 10 seedlings
   (D) 4 seedlings

8. How much solution do you need if you are asked for $\frac{7}{10}$ of 50 mL of solution?

   (F) 7 mL
   (G) 40 mL
   (H) 35 mL
   (J) 42 mL

Science

| S4SC3 |

Lab Safety

DIRECTIONS: Read the following statements about behaviors in a science lab. Indicate whether the behavior is safe **(S)** or unsafe **(U)**.

_____ 1. You will be in the lab for a while. Bring food and drink with you so you have something to eat and drink while you are conducting your experiments.

_____ 2. Thoroughly clean all work surfaces and equipment after each use.

_____ 3. Wear closed-toe shoes when conducting experiments with liquids or with heated or heavy items.

_____ 4. Have some fun with fellow classmates when you are waiting for liquids to boil. A little horseplay will make the experiment seem to go faster.

_____ 5. Use mouth suction when filling pipettes with chemicals.

_____ 6. Make certain all hot plates and burners are turned off before leaving the lab.

_____ 7. Avoid transferring chemicals to your face, hands, or other areas of exposed skin.

_____ 8. You do not need to wash your hands after coming into contact with plant, soil, or water samples as contamination is not possible.

_____ 9. It is okay to use chemicals that are past their expiration date. Reactions may just take a little longer.

_____ 10. If you are asked to use your sense of smell during an experiment, waft the vapors toward your nose using your hand. Do not inhale vapors directly.

STOP

Displaying Data

DIRECTIONS: Ramon and Lila are studying weather. They recorded the following average daily temperature in Macon for the past week. In the space below, construct a bar graph to represent the data. Then indicate whether the pattern of change is *steady, repetitive,* or *irregular.*

Day	Temperature (°F)
Sunday	70°
Monday	72°
Tuesday	69°
Wednesday	74°
Thursday	80°
Friday	91°
Saturday	77°

The pattern of change shown here is _____ .

STOP

Name _____ Date _____

Locating Information

DIRECTIONS: Your teacher wants you to find information on glaciers. Conduct your research on this topic using a variety of sources, such as encyclopedias, books, scientific journals, newspapers, magazines, and the Internet. In the spaces below, list your five sources and briefly describe the type of information included in each one.

Source 1: _____

Description of information: _____

_____

_____

_____

Source 2: _____

Description of information: _____

_____

_____

_____

Source 3: _____

Description of information: _____

_____

_____

_____

Source 4: _____

Description of information: _____

_____

_____

_____

Source 5: _____

Description of information: _____

_____

_____

_____

STOP

Science

S4CS6

Using Data to Support Statements

DIRECTIONS: Read the passage, and then answer the questions.

Planet Temperatures

Scientists have looked at the other planets in our solar system to see if they would be good places to live. One of the first problems is temperature. Earth's average temperature is about 58°F, which is the temperature on a brisk fall day. Our neighbor Venus is one planet closer to the sun than Earth and much hotter. The average temperature on Venus is 867°F. This is mostly because of Venus's thick atmosphere, which traps the sun's heat so that it cannot escape. The trapping of heat in this way is called the *greenhouse effect.* It is named for the way that hot air is trapped inside a greenhouse and is kept warmer than the air outside. On the other hand, Earth's neighbor Mars is one planet farther away from the sun. It's a little too cold for comfort on Mars. Its average temperature is about –65°F.

1. **What is the greenhouse effect?**

   (A) air that is trapped by glass and cannot escape

   (B) air that is heated by the sun and then trapped by a planet's thick atmosphere

   (C) air that is heated by the sun and then orbits a planet and keeps it warm

   (D) air that travels from one planet to another

2. **Which of these might be an example of the greenhouse effect?**

   (F) a car on a summer's day with the air conditioning on

   (G) a parked car on a summer's day with the windows closed

   (H) a car on a summer's day that is traveling down the highway with the windows open

   (J) a parked car on a summer's day with all of the windows open

3. **After reading the passage, which of these statements do you think is probably true?**

   (A) The average temperature increases the closer a planet is to the sun.

   (B) The average temperature increases the closer a planet is to Earth.

   (C) The average temperature decreases the closer a planet is to the sun.

   (D) The average temperature increases the farther a planet is from the sun.

4. **After reading the passage, which conclusion can you draw?**

   (F) With the proper shelter, it would be possible to live on Mars.

   (G) With the proper shelter, it would be possible to live on Venus.

   (H) Earth's average temperature is colder than Mars' average temperature.

   (J) Earth's average temperature is warmer than Venus's average temperature.

Science

Science | S4CS1–S4CS6

For pages 161–166

Mini-Test 1

Habits of Mind

DIRECTIONS: Choose the best answer.

1. Jan read an article about how the dinosaurs became extinct. It said that most scientists agreed that at some time in the past a huge asteroid had hit Earth. This caused certain environmental changes that made it difficult for dinosaurs to survive. Scientists have several hypotheses about how the asteroid killed off the dinosaurs. Which of the following seems most likely?

   (A) It caused an ice age.

   (B) It caused fires that destroyed food dinosaurs needed to survive.

   (C) It caused "space sickness."

   (D) It turned the dinosaurs to stone.

2. You mix 300 mL of a solution. The next step in your experiment calls for transferring $\frac{2}{5}$ of this solution into another container. How much solution will you need to remove from the original amount?

   (F) 60 mL

   (G) 90 mL

   (H) 120 mL

   (J) 180 mL

3. Which of the following is another way of recording $\frac{2}{5}$?

   (A) 0.25

   (B) 0.4

   (C) 0.6

   (D) 2.50

4. Which of the following is *not* an example of using safety precautions in a science lab?

   (F) Wear a protective apron.

   (G) Use your bare hands to handle hot materials.

   (H) Keep personal items off the lab tables.

   (J) Wash your hands after you are finished.

5. Which of the following safety items should you make sure to have in a science lab?

   (A) rubber or latex gloves

   (B) chemical splash goggles

   (C) first-aid kit

   (D) all of the above

6. Study the following chart showing the times that Venus will rise over the next five days. Which type of pattern of change does the chart illustrate?

Day	Time that Venus will rise
Sunday	6:24 A.M.
Monday	6:20 A.M.
Tuesday	6:16 A.M.
Wednesday	6:12 A.M.
Thursday	6:08 A.M.

   (F) irregular

   (G) steady

   (H) repetitive

   (J) none of the above

STOP

The Nature of Science Standards

S4CS7. Students will be familiar with the character of scientific knowledge and how it is achieved. *(See page 169.)* **Students will recognize the following concepts.**

a. Similar scientific investigations seldom produce exactly the same results, which may differ due to unexpected differences in whatever is being investigated, unrecognized differences in methods or circumstances of the investigation, or observational uncertainties.

b. Some scientific knowledge is very old and yet is still applicable today.

S4CS8. Students will understand important features of the process of scientific inquiry. *(See page 170.)* **Students will apply the following to inquiry learning practices.**

a. Scientific investigations may take many different forms, including observing what things are like or what is happening somewhere, collecting specimens for analysis, and doing experiments.

b. Clear and active communication is an essential part of doing science. It enables scientists to inform others about their work, expose their ideas to criticism by other scientists, and stay informed about scientific discoveries around the world.

c. Scientists use technology to increase their power to observe things and to measure and compare things accurately.

d. Science involves many different kinds of work and engages men and women of all ages and backgrounds.

Name _____ Date _____

S4CS7

Scientific Results and Knowledge

DIRECTIONS: Read the text and then answer the question.

Clue

Similar scientific investigations seldom get the exact same results. This can be due to unexpected differences in what is being investigated or differences in the way the investigation is carried out.

Terry wanted to chart how much his flower seeds would grow in a month. In August, he planted the seeds and placed the seedlings on a windowsill that faced south. As soon as they sprouted, he carefully measured the flowers and recorded their measurements every day for the next month. Here is part of his log for the first experiment.

Day 1:   planted the flower seedlings and placed them on a windowsill that faced south.
Day 14:   The seedlings have begun to sprout.
Day 16:   Plant One measures 1 cm; Plant Two measures 1.2 cm.
Day 44:   Plant One measures 21 cm; Plant Two measures 22 cm.

He repeated the same experiment in September, using the same location and the same flowers seeds that he had used in the first experiment. Here is part of his log for the second experiment.

Day 1:   planted the flower seedlings and placed them on a windowsill that faced south.
Day 18:   The seedlings have begun to sprout.
Day 20:   Plant One measures 0.7 cm; Plant Two measures 1 cm.
Day 48:   Plant One measures 19 cm; Plant Two measures 19.5 cm.

During the second experiment, the seeds sprouted a few days later than the seeds in the first experiment. What could have caused this?

_____

_____

_____

_____

_____

_____

STOP

Science

| S4CS8 |

Scientific Inquiry

Clue

- When you use *observation,* you are watching what is happening. You are not creating the event.
- When you *collect specimens,* you are collecting items to be studied.
- When you *perform an experiment,* you are actively involved in finding an answer to a question. For example, what will happen if you add baking soda to vinegar? Since the baking soda cannot add itself naturally, you must add it. Therefore, you are creating the event.

DIRECTIONS: Choose the best answer.

1. **Which of the following types of investigation would you use to determine the effects of using fertilizer on plants?**
   - (A) observation
   - (B) collecting specimens
   - (C) doing experiments
   - (D) all of the above

2. **Which of the following types of investigation would you use to determine how much snow is received in a given month?**
   - (F) observation
   - (G) collecting specimens
   - (H) doing experiments
   - (J) all of the above

3. **Which of the following types of investigation would you use to determine what types of fossils are contained in rocks in your area?**
   - (A) observation
   - (B) collecting specimens
   - (C) doing experiments
   - (D) all of the above

4. **Which of the following would you use to determine which of two objects is heavier?**
   - (F) a ruler
   - (G) a balance scale
   - (H) a barometer
   - (J) a beaker

5. **Which of the following would you use for measuring liquids in a science lab?**
   - (A) a graduated cylinder
   - (B) a beaker
   - (C) a Petri dish
   - (D) a test tube

6. **A person who studies water and its properties is a _____ .**
   - (F) seismologist
   - (G) zoologist
   - (H) geneticist
   - (J) hydrologist

7. **A person who studies animals is a _____ .**
   - (A) geneticist
   - (B) paleontologist
   - (C) zoologist
   - (D) geologist

8. **A person who studies earthquakes is a(n) _____ .**
   - (F) seismologist
   - (G) hydrologist
   - (H) paleontologist
   - (J) entomologist

Science

S4CS7–S4CS8

For pages 169–170

Mini-Test 2

The Nature
of Science

DIRECTIONS: Choose the best answer.

1. **Which of the following types of investigation would you use to determine what type of nest sea turtles build?**
   - (A) observation
   - (B) collecting specimens
   - (C) doing experiments
   - (D) all of the above

2. **Which of the following types of investigation would you use to determine what happens when you add hot water to ice?**
   - (F) observation
   - (G) doing experiments
   - (H) collecting specimens
   - (J) all of the above

3. **Which of the following types of investigation would you use to determine if microorganisms are found in your drinking water?**
   - (A) collecting specimens
   - (B) observation
   - (C) doing experiments
   - (D) all of the above

4. **A person who studies fossils is a(n) _____ .**
   - (F) paleontologist
   - (G) entomologist
   - (H) zoologist
   - (J) microbiologist

5. **A seismologist is someone who studies _____ .**
   - (A) water and its properties
   - (B) animals
   - (C) earthquakes
   - (D) how traits are inherited

6. **A zoologist is someone who studies _____ .**
   - (F) insects
   - (G) fossils
   - (H) earthquakes
   - (J) animals

7. **Which of the following would you use to study organisms in a drop of water?**
   - (A) a telescope
   - (B) a microscope
   - (C) a magnifying glass
   - (D) a bifocal lens

8. **Which of the following would you use to determine which runs faster—a dog or a cat?**
   - (F) a ruler
   - (G) a stopwatch
   - (H) a barometer
   - (J) an odometer

9. **Which of the following would you use to determine if a solution is an acid or a base?**
   - (A) litmus paper
   - (B) construction paper
   - (C) a microscope
   - (D) a telescope

STOP

Earth Science Standards

S4E1. Students will compare and contrast the physical attributes of stars, star patterns, and planets. *(See page 173.)*
   a. Recognize the physical attributes of stars in the night sky such as number, size, color, and patterns.
   b. Compare the similarities and differences of planets to the stars in appearance, position, and number in the night sky.
   c. Explain why the pattern of stars in a constellation stays the same, but a planet can be seen in different locations at different times.
   d. Identify how technology is used to observe distant objects in the sky.

S4E2. Students will model the position and motion of Earth in the solar system and will explain the role of relative position and motion in determining sequence of the phases of the moon. *(See pages 174–175.)*
   a. Explain the day/night cycle of Earth using a model.
   b. Explain the sequence of the phases of the moon.
   c. Demonstrate the revolution of Earth around the sun and Earth's tilt to explain the seasonal changes.
   d. Demonstrate the relative size and order from the sun of the planets in the solar system.

S4E3. Students will differentiate between the states of water and how they relate to the water cycle and weather. *(See page 176.)*
   a. Demonstrate how water changes states from solid (ice) to liquid (water) to gas (water vapor/steam) and changes from gas to liquid to solid.
   b. Identify the temperatures at which water becomes a solid and at which water becomes a gas.
   c. Investigate how clouds are formed.
   d. Explain the water cycle (evaporation, condensation, and precipitation).
   e. Investigate different forms of precipitation and sky conditions (rain, snow, sleet, hail, clouds, and fog).

S4E4. Students will analyze weather charts/maps and collect weather data to predict weather events and infer patterns and seasonal changes. *(See page 177.)*
   a. Identify weather instruments and explain how each is used in gathering weather data and making forecasts (thermometer, rain gauge, barometer, wind vane, anemometer).
   b. Using a weather map, identify the fronts, temperature, and precipitation and use the information to interpret the weather conditions.
   c. Use the observations and records of weather conditions to predict weather patterns throughout the year.
   d. Differentiate between weather and climate.

S4E1

Constellations

DIRECTIONS: Match the constellations pictured below with their names.

Constellations

A the Big Dipper
B Orion
C Cassiopeia
D Cygnus
E Cepheus

1. _____

4. _____

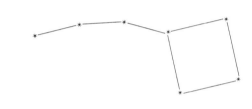

2. _____

5. _____

3. _____

STOP

S4E2

Patterns in the Solid System
Patterns in the Solar System

DIRECTIONS: Read the selection. Choose the best answer.

Why Are There Seasons?

Earth revolves around the sun. It also spins on an invisible axis that runs through its center.

It takes $365\frac{1}{4}$ days, or one year, for Earth to revolve once around the sun. Just as the moon moves in an orbit around Earth, Earth moves around the sun. Earth does not move in a perfect circle. Its orbit is an ellipse, which is a flattened circle, like an oval. As Earth revolves around the sun in an elliptical shape, it spins on its invisible axis.

Earth's axis of rotation is not straight up and down; it is tilted. This important feature produces the seasons on Earth. No matter where Earth is in its rotation around the sun, its axis is tilted in the same direction and at the same angle. So, as Earth moves, different parts of it are facing the sun and different parts are facing away. The North Pole is tilting toward the sun in June, so the northern half of Earth is enjoying summer. In December, the North Pole is tilted away from the sun, so the northern part of the world experiences winter.

This important relationship between Earth and the sun determines how hot and cold we are, when we plant our crops, and whether we have droughts or floods.

1. **If North America is having summer, what season would the Australians be enjoying?**

   Ⓐ spring

   Ⓑ summer

   Ⓒ winter

   Ⓓ fall

2. **What would happen if Earth's axis were not tilted, but straight up and down?**

   Ⓕ Nothing would change.

   Ⓖ Earth wouldn't change seasons.

   Ⓗ It would always be summer on Earth.

   Ⓙ It would always be winter on Earth.

DIRECTIONS: Choose the best answer.

3. **Picture A shows the moon as it looked on August 1. Picture B shows the moon as it looked on August 14. Which of the following shows how the moon will look on August 28?**

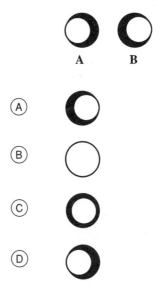

4. **What causes the sun to appear to rise and set?**

   Ⓕ Earth's revolution

   Ⓖ the sun's revolution

   Ⓗ Earth's rotation

   Ⓙ Earth's elliptical orbit

Science   **Earth Science**

S4E2

Planets in the
Solar System

DIRECTIONS: Fill in the blanks with the names of planets according to their correct order from the sun.

1. _____

2. _____

3. _____

4. _____

5. _____

6. _____

7. _____

8. _____

9. _____

STOP

Science

Earth Science

S4E3

Properties of Water

DIRECTIONS: Choose the best answer.

1. Ice is water in its _____ state.
   - (A) solid
   - (B) changing
   - (C) liquid
   - (D) gas

2. When water freezes, it changes from a _____ .
   - (F) gas to a solid
   - (G) liquid to a gas
   - (H) liquid to a solid
   - (J) solid to a gas

3. Malcom left a cube of ice in a glass on a window sill. In about an hour, the ice changed into a clear substance that took on the shape of the lower part of the glass. Finally, after three days, there appeared to be nothing in the glass at all. What states of matter did the ice cube pass through?
   - (A) liquid then gas then solid
   - (B) solid then liquid then gas
   - (C) gas then liquid then solid
   - (D) solid then gas then liquid

4. At which temperature does water become a solid?
   - (F) 32°C
   - (G) 0°F
   - (H) 32°F
   - (J) 100°C

5. The water cycle occurs between the earth and the _____ .
   - (A) hydrosphere
   - (B) atmosphere
   - (C) stratosphere
   - (D) biosphere

6. Which of the following has the least effect on the water cycle?
   - (F) temperature
   - (G) air pressure
   - (H) land features
   - (J) soil

7. Water vapor forming droplets that form clouds directly involves which process?
   - (A) condensation
   - (B) precipitation
   - (C) evaporation
   - (D) transpiration

8. In the water cycle, how is water returned to the atmosphere?
   - (F) evaporation
   - (G) condensation
   - (H) precipitation
   - (J) fixation

9. A rainstorm is an example of _____ .
   - (A) precipitation
   - (B) evaporation
   - (C) condensation
   - (D) respiration

10. When a puddle of water disappears after the sun comes out, it is called _____ .
    - (F) precipitation
    - (G) transpiration
    - (H) condensation
    - (J) evaporation

| S4E4 | **Weather**

DIRECTIONS: Choose the best answer.

1. **Which of the following instruments would you use to determine how fast the wind is blowing?**
   - (A) a wind vane
   - (B) a barometer
   - (C) an anemometer
   - (D) a thermometer

2. **Which of the following instruments would you use to measure air pressure?**
   - (F) an anemometer
   - (G) a wind vane
   - (H) a thermometer
   - (J) a barometer

3. **What does a rain gauge measure?**
   - (A) the amount of rainfall
   - (B) the intensity of rainfall
   - (C) the anticipated rainfall
   - (D) the duration of rainfall

4. **A cold front on a weather map is indicated by _____ .**
   - (F) a blue line with triangles pointing in the direction that the cold air is moving
   - (G) a blue line with semicircles pointing in the direction that the cold air is moving
   - (H) a red line with triangles pointing in the direction that the cold air is moving
   - (J) a red line with semicircles pointing in the direction that the cold air is moving

5. **Warm, low-pressure air can hold more water than cold air. As warm air rises, it cools. This causes water vapor to gather together, or condense, into water drops. What kind of weather probably goes along with low air pressure?**
   - (A) clouds and rain
   - (B) clouds without rain
   - (C) clear skies
   - (D) tornadoes

6. **Climate is different from weather in that it _____ .**
   - (F) changes more rapidly
   - (G) changes less rapidly
   - (H) is more extreme
   - (J) is reported daily on local television news

7. **Study the table below. Which month is likely to have the most hurricanes?**
   - (A) July
   - (B) August
   - (C) September
   - (D) October

Month Formed	Tropical Storms	Hurricanes
January–April	4	1
May	14	3
June	57	23
July	68	35
August	221	?
September	311	?
October	188	?
November	42	22
December	6	3

STOP

Science

S4E1–S4E4

For pages 173–177

Mini-Test 3

DIRECTIONS: Choose the best answer.

1. **Patterns made by stars in the night sky are called _____ .**
   - (A) constellations
   - (B) galaxies
   - (C) nebulas
   - (D) comets

2. **What is the largest planet in our solar system?**
   - (F) Earth
   - (G) Neptune
   - (H) Jupiter
   - (J) Saturn

3. **Study the chart below and determine what the moon phase will be during week 6.**

   - (A)
   - (B)
   - (C)
   - (D)

4. **One morning you wake up and find dew on the yard. Throughout the day, the weather is hot and sunny. Later that day, you notice that the dew is gone. This is an example of _____ .**
   - (F) condensation
   - (G) evaporation
   - (H) precipitation
   - (J) transpiration

5. **In the water cycle, how does water reach the earth?**
   - (A) condensation
   - (B) evaporation
   - (C) precipitation
   - (D) transpiration

6. **How long does it take for Earth to complete one rotation on its axis?**
   - (F) one hour
   - (G) one day
   - (H) one week
   - (J) one month

7. **Which of the following instruments tells you in which direction the wind is blowing?**
   - (A) an anemometer
   - (B) a barometer
   - (C) a wind vane
   - (D) a thermometer

8. **It is a spring day in Georgia with a temperature of 70°F. The weather forecaster is predicting precipitation. What are you most likely to see?**
   - (F) rain
   - (G) snow
   - (H) sleet
   - (J) none of the above

Physical Science Standards

S4P1. Students will investigate the nature of light using tools such as mirrors, lenses, and prisms. *(See page 180.)*
a. Identify materials that are transparent, opaque, and translucent.
b. Investigate the reflection of light using a mirror and a light source.
c. Identify the physical attributes of a convex lens, a concave lens, and a prism and where each is used.

S4P2. Students will demonstrate how sound is produced by vibrating objects and how sound can be varied by changing the rate of vibration. *(See page 181.)*
a. Investigate how sound is produced.
b. Recognize the conditions that cause pitch to vary.

S4P3. Students will demonstrate the relationship between the application of a force and the resulting change in position and motion on an object. *(See page 182.)*
a. Identify simple machines and explain their uses (lever, pulley, wedge, inclined plane, screw, wheel and axle).
b. Using different-sized objects, observe how force affects speed and motion.
c. Explain what happens to the speed or direction of an object when a greater force than the initial one is applied.
d. Demonstrate the effect of gravitational force on the motion of an object.
Teacher note: The use of mathematical formulas is not recommended in S4P3. Fourth-grade students should carry out investigations to provide a foundation of concrete experience for abstract understandings of physical science in upper grades.

Science   **Physical Science**

| S4P1 |

Light

DIRECTIONS: Choose the best answer.

1. **A translucent object is one in which** _____ .
   - (A) light can travel through undistorted
   - (B) some light can travel through
   - (C) no light can travel through
   - (D) none of the above

2. **An opaque object is one in which** _____ .
   - (F) no light can travel through
   - (G) light can travel through undistorted
   - (H) some light can travel through
   - (J) none of the above

3. **A transparent object is one in which** _____ .
   - (A) some light can travel through
   - (B) no light can travel through
   - (C) light can travel through undistorted
   - (D) none of the above

4. **Which of the following items is translucent?**
   - (F) cardboard
   - (G) tissue paper
   - (H) construction paper
   - (J) clear glass

5. **Which of the following items is transparent?**
   - (A) eye glasses
   - (B) stained glass
   - (C) tin foil
   - (D) a brick wall

6. **Which of the following has a thick center and thinner edges?**
   - (F) concave lens
   - (G) convex lens
   - (H) straight lens
   - (J) curved lens

7. **Which of the following has a thinner middle than the edges?**
   - (A) mirror
   - (B) prism
   - (C) convex lens
   - (D) concave lens

8. **What tool would you use to split white light into colors?**
   - (F) a mirror
   - (G) a prism
   - (H) a convex lens
   - (J) a concave lens

9. **Which of the following is used in a magnifying glass?**
   - (A) a prism
   - (B) a concave lens
   - (C) a mirror
   - (D) a convex lens

STOP

180

Science

S4P2

Sound

DIRECTIONS: Read about Miranda's experiment and then answer questions 1–4.

Miranda made two drums. For Drum A, she covered a large, empty coffee can with wax paper and fastened the paper with tape. For Drum B, she covered a small, empty soup can with wax paper and fastened the paper with tape. Then she firmly beat on the surface of each drum.

1. **What statement is probably true?**
   - (A) Drum A has a lower tone.
   - (B) Drum B has a lower tone.
   - (C) Drums A and B have the same tone.
   - (D) Drum A has a higher tone.

2. **If Miranda beat one drum more quickly, its sound waves would become _____ .**
   - (F) farther apart
   - (G) closer together
   - (H) shorter
   - (J) longer

3. **How do the sound waves of lower tones differ from the sound waves of higher tones?**
   - (A) They are longer.
   - (B) They are shorter.
   - (C) They are closer together.
   - (D) They are farther apart.

4. **In which situation could sound not travel?**
   - (F) through a wood and plaster wall
   - (G) in the water
   - (H) in a vacuum
   - (J) through the air

DIRECTIONS: Choose the best answer.

5. **When you wear earplugs, you can't hear because the vibrations cannot reach your _____ .**
   - (A) air
   - (B) eardrums
   - (C) ear canal
   - (D) medium

6. **For the vocal cords to produce a _____ pitch, they must get tighter and closer together.**
   - (F) high
   - (G) loud
   - (H) low
   - (J) soft

7. **A piano tuner will tighten the strings of a piano so that the pitch will be _____ .**
   - (A) louder
   - (B) softer
   - (C) lower
   - (D) higher

8. **Bats and dolphins both hear a _____ than humans do.**
   - (F) smaller range of pitches
   - (G) smaller range of frequencies
   - (H) larger range of resonances
   - (J) larger range of pitches and frequencies

STOP

Science

Physical Science

S4P3

Simple Machines

DIRECTIONS: Choose the best answer.

1. **A chisel is an example of what type of simple machine?**
    - (A) an inclined plane
    - (B) a lever
    - (C) a wedge
    - (D) a pulley

2. **A wheelchair ramp is an example of what type of simple machine?**
    - (F) a wedge
    - (G) an inclined plane
    - (H) a lever
    - (J) a pulley

3. **Which of the following simple machines makes up the base of a lightbulb?**
    - (A) wheel and axle
    - (B) lever
    - (C) screw
    - (D) pulley

4. **What simple machine gives the unicycle its ability to travel?**
    - (F) a wheel and axle
    - (G) a screw
    - (H) an inclined plane
    - (J) a pulley

5. **A seesaw is an example of what type of simple machine?**
    - (A) a wedge
    - (B) a wheel and axle
    - (C) an inclined plane
    - (D) a lever

6. **Movers are trying to load furniture into their moving van. The simple machine that would be most useful would be a(n) _____ .**
    - (F) wedge
    - (G) inclined plane
    - (H) lever
    - (J) wheel and axle

7. **Children are trying to get supplies up to their tree house. The simple machine that would be most useful to them would be a _____ .**
    - (A) pulley
    - (B) lever
    - (C) wheel and axle
    - (D) screw

8   **A back of the head of a hammer is useful for removing nails from wood. This is an example of what type of machine?**
    - (F) a lever
    - (G) a wedge
    - (H) an inclined plane
    - (J) a wheel and axle

9. **Your dad is using an ax to split some logs. What type of simple machine is he using to accomplish this task?**
    - (A) a screw
    - (B) a wedge
    - (C) a pulley
    - (D) a lever

Science

Physical Science

| S4P1–S4P3 |

Mini-Test 4

For pages 180–182

DIRECTIONS: Choose the best answer.

1. **You have a frosted glass shower door installed in your bathroom. Which of the following terms would you use to describe the door?**
    - (A) opaque
    - (B) translucent
    - (C) transparent
    - (D) obscure

2. **Your neighbors install a picket fence behind their garden. Which of the following terms describes the picket fence?**
    - (F) translucent
    - (G) transparent
    - (H) opaque
    - (J) light

3. **Light passing through which of the following items is bent inward, or converges?**
    - (A) a prism
    - (B) a mirror
    - (C) a concave lens
    - (D) a convex lens

4. **What type of lens is used to correct nearsightedness?**
    - (F) round
    - (G) flat
    - (H) convex
    - (J) concave

5. **A doorknob is an example of what type of simple machine?**
    - (A) lever
    - (B) pulley
    - (C) wheel and axle
    - (D) screw

6. **A doorstop is an example of what type of simple machine?**
    - (F) a wedge
    - (G) an inclined plane
    - (H) a lever
    - (J) a pulley

7. **You are trying to raise a flag up a flagpole. The simple machine that would be most useful would be a(n) _____ .**
    - (A) inclined plane
    - (B) screw
    - (C) pulley
    - (D) wheel and axle

8. **The Egyptians built large pyramids. What simple machine did they most likely use to move the bricks up to the top of the pyramid?**
    - (F) a lever
    - (G) an inclined plane
    - (H) a wheel and axle
    - (J) a wedge

STOP

Life Science Standards

S4L1. Students will describe the roles of organisms and the flow of energy within an ecosystem. *(See page 185.)*
a. Identify the roles of producers, consumers, and decomposers in a community.
b. Demonstrate the flow of energy through a food web/food chain beginning with sunlight and including producers, consumers, and decomposers.
c. Predict how changes in the environment would affect a community (ecosystem) of organisms.
d. Predict effects on a population if some of the plants or animals in the community are scarce or if there are too many.

S4L2. Students will identify factors that affect the survival or extinction of organisms such as adaptation, variation of behaviors (hibernation), and external features (camouflage and protection). *(See page 186.)*
a. Identify external features of organisms that allow them to survive or reproduce better than organisms that do not have these features (e.g., camouflage, use of hibernation, protection, etc.).
b. Identify factors that may have led to the extinction of some organisms.

Science   **Life Science**

| S4L1 | # Organisms in Ecosystems

DIRECTIONS: Choose the best answer.

1. An organism that lives by feeding on other organisms is called a _____ .
   - (A) producer
   - (B) consumer
   - (C) decomposer
   - (D) none of the above

2. An organism, usually a green plant, which can make its own food is called a _____ .
   - (F) consumer
   - (G) decomposer
   - (H) producer
   - (J) none of the above

3. An organism that feeds on the remains of other organisms is called a _____ .
   - (A) decomposer
   - (B) producer
   - (C) consumer
   - (D) none of the above

4. In a predator-prey relationship, when the predator population increases, the prey population will probably _____ .
   - (F) increase
   - (G) decrease
   - (H) stay the same
   - (J) not enough information to know

5. In a predator-prey relationship, when the prey population increases, the predator population will probably _____ .
   - (A) increase
   - (B) decrease
   - (C) stay the same
   - (D) not enough information to know

6. If the temperature in a warm region, such as a desert, suddenly dropped by 50 degrees, what types of organisms might completely die out?

   _____

   _____

   _____

   _____

   _____

   _____

7. Which organisms would thrive in a colder environment? What challenges might they still face?

   _____

   _____

   _____

   _____

   _____

   _____

STOP

Science

| S4L2 |

Life Science

Adaptive Characteristics

DIRECTIONS: Match the ecosystem of each mystery organism in **Column A** to one or more adaptations that would be most beneficial for its survival in **Column B**.

COLUMN A

1. _____ **in a tree in the rainforest**

2. _____ **underground in the backyard**

3. _____ **on the leaves of a rose bush**

4. _____ **in a coral reef**

5. _____ **on a glacier in Alaska**

6. _____ **on a mountainside**

7. _____ **in a polluted stream**

8. _____ **in the desert**

9. _____ **on the side of a cliff**

10. _____ **in a cave**

11. _____ **in a forest in the midwest**

12. _____ **on the bank of a nearly dry stream**

COLUMN B

a. strong legs for climbing

b. a tail to help it hang from branches

c. deep roots to find water

d. the ability to breathe air as well as water

e. being a color that blends in with leaves

f. strong claws for digging and moving dirt

g. a thick coat and layer of fat

h. strong wings to fly and glide

i. ability to see in the dark

j. clear eyelids to keep out sand and dirt

k. hibernating in the winter when food is scarce

l. ability to completely draw inside a shell

STOP

Science   **Life Science**

| S4L1–S4L2 |

For pages 185–186

Mini-Test 5

DIRECTIONS: Identify each organism by writing *producer, consumer,* or *decomposer* in the blank following its name.

1. cactus _____

2. lion _____

3. bacterium _____

4. cow _____

5. blue whale _____

6. grass _____

7. earthworm _____

8. fir tree _____

DIRECTIONS: Choose the best answer.

9. **Which level of the food chain has the most energy?**
   - (A) decomposers
   - (B) producers
   - (C) consumers
   - (D) They each have the same amount of energy.

10. **A trait or ability that helps an organism survive in its environment is called a(n) _____ .**
    - (F) response
    - (G) adaptation
    - (H) ecosystem
    - (J) organization

11. **An adaptation related to a fox's keen sense of hearing is the fox's _____ .**
    - (A) long, bushy tail
    - (B) long snout
    - (C) large, upright ears
    - (D) sharp, canine teeth

12. **A chameleon's ability to change its color to blend in with its surroundings is an adaptation called _____ .**
    - (F) selection
    - (G) symmetry
    - (H) evolution
    - (J) camouflage

13. **An example of camouflage is _____ .**
    - (A) a tiger's stripes
    - (B) a bird's beak
    - (C) a porcupine's quills
    - (D) a monkey's tail

STOP

How Am I Doing?

Mini-Test 1 Page 167 **Number Correct**	**6** answers correct	**Great Job!** Move on to the section test on page 190.
	5 answers correct	**You're almost there!** But you still need a little practice. Review practice pages 161–166 before moving on to the section test on page 190.
	0–4 answers correct	**Oops!** Time to review what you have learned and try again. Review the practice section on pages 161–166. Then retake the test on page 167. Now move on to the section test on page 190.
Mini-Test 2 Page 171 **Number Correct**	**8–9** answers correct	**Awesome!** Move on to the section test on page 190.
	5–7 answers correct	**You're almost there!** But you still need a little practice. Review practice pages 169–170 before moving on to the section test on page 190.
	0–4 answers correct	**Oops!** Time to review what you have learned and try again. Review the practice section on pages 169–170. Then retake the test on page 171. Now move on to the section test on page 190.
Mini-Test 3 Page 178 **Number Correct**	**8** answers correct	**Great Job!** Move on to the section test on page 190.
	5–7 answers correct	**You're almost there!** But you still need a little practice. Review practice pages 173–177 before moving on to the section test on page 190.
	0–4 answers correct	**Oops!** Time to review what you have learned and try again. Review the practice section on pages 173–177. Then retake the test on page 178. Now move on to the section test on page 190.

How Am I Doing?

Mini-Test 4	8 answers correct	**Awesome!** Move on to the section test on page 190.
Page 183 **Number Correct**	5–7 answers correct	**You're almost there!** But you still need a little practice. Review practice pages 180–182 before moving on to the section test on page 190.
	0–4 answers correct	**Oops!** Time to review what you have learned and try again. Review the practice section on pages 180–182. Then retake the test on page 183. Now move on to the section test on page 190.
Mini-Test 5	11–13 answers correct	**Great Job!** Move on to the section test on page 190.
Page 187 **Number Correct**	7–10 answers correct	**You're almost there!** But you still need a little practice. Review practice pages 185–186 before moving on to the section test on page 190.
	0–6 answers correct	**Oops!** Time to review what you have learned and try again. Review the practice section on pages 185–186. Then retake the test on page 187. Now move on to the section test on page 190.

Final Science Test
for pages 161–187

DIRECTIONS: Choose the best answer.

1. Miguel watched as several fruit flies buzzed around the bananas on the counter. He wondered where they came from since it was very cold outside and they only live for 24 hours. Which of the following is a strong theory for how the fruit flies got on the bananas?

   (A) Fruit fly eggs were on the bananas when his mother bought them.

   (B) The fruit flies were hiding in the house since summer.

   (C) Bananas turn into fruit flies as they ripen.

   (D) When bananas are near apples, fruit flies appear.

2. Carol wanted to learn more about how the greenhouse effect affects particular ecosystems, so she created a mini-ecosystem of her own. She got a large glass container and filled it halfway with soil. She put in leaves and twigs. Then she replanted some small plants from her garden. Finally, she added a few earthworms, some beetles, and a butterfly cocoon. If the plants die and the cocoon does not hatch, what could Carol conclude?

   (F) The greenhouse effect has no effect on her ecosystem.

   (G) She did a bad job of taking care of her plants and animals.

   (H) The greenhouse effect has a negative effect on her ecosystem.

   (J) The greenhouse effect has a positive effect on her ecosystem.

3. How would you record $\frac{45}{100}$ in decimal notation?

   (A) 45

   (B) 4.5

   (C) 0.45

   (D) 0.045

4. You mix 850 mL of a solution. You are asked to transfer $\frac{1}{5}$ of this solution to one container and $\frac{2}{5}$ to a second container. How much solution will you measure out into the first container?

   (F) 510 mL

   (G) 340 mL

   (H) 170 mL

   (J) 680 mL

5. After transferring all of the solution to the two containers in question 4, how much will remain in the original container?

   (A) 340 mL

   (B) 510 mL

   (C) 680 mL

   (D) 170 mL

6. Which of the following is *not* a safety behavior in the lab?

   (F) tying back long hair

   (G) using chemicals that are beyond their expiration date

   (H) wearing safety goggles

   (J) wearing a protective apron

7. Which of the following types of investigation would you use to determine the effects of sunlight versus artificial light on plants?

   (A) observation

   (B) collecting specimens

   (C) doing experiments

   (D) all of the above

8. **What does a geneticist study?**

   Ⓕ plants

   Ⓖ how traits are inherited

   Ⓗ fossils

   Ⓙ cells

9. **A person who studies microscopic plants and animals is a _____ .**

   Ⓐ marine biologist

   Ⓑ botanist

   Ⓒ zoologist

   Ⓓ microbiologist

10. **The Big Dipper is a type of _____ .**

   Ⓕ constellation

   Ⓖ galaxy

   Ⓗ star cluster

   Ⓙ nebula

11. **Study the chart below. What will the moon phase probably be on March 27?**

Date	Moon Phase
December 29	Full moon
January 5	Last quarter
January 11	New moon
January 19	First quarter
January 27	Full moon
February 3	Last quarter
February 10	New moon
February 18	First quarter
February 26	Full moon

   Ⓐ full moon

   Ⓑ last quarter

   Ⓒ new moon

   Ⓓ first quarter

12. **Which planet is closest to the sun?**

   Ⓕ Mars

   Ⓖ Mercury

   Ⓗ Pluto

   Ⓙ Venus

13. **When water melts from an ice cube, the water changes from a _____ .**

   Ⓐ solid to a gas

   Ⓑ liquid to a vapor

   Ⓒ solid to a liquid

   Ⓓ liquid to a solid

14. **At which temperature does water become a gas?**

   Ⓕ 100°C

   Ⓖ 0°C

   Ⓗ 212°C

   Ⓙ 32°C

15. **Which of the following is *not* part of the water cycle?**

   Ⓐ evaporation

   Ⓑ condensation

   Ⓒ precipitation

   Ⓓ respiration

16. **Which of the following is a form of precipitation?**

   Ⓕ rain

   Ⓖ snow

   Ⓗ sleet

   Ⓙ all of the above

17. **What does a barometer measure?**

   Ⓐ wind speed

   Ⓑ temperature

   Ⓒ air pressure

   Ⓓ wind direction

GO

18. On a weather map, a red line with semicircles indicates _____ .

(F) a cold front

(G) a warm front

(H) low air pressure

(J) high air pressure

19. A weather front passed through the state of Georgia today. Low-pressure air moved off to the east and was replaced by high-pressure air from the west. What kind of weather is most likely to occur in Georgia tomorrow?

(A) thunderstorms

(B) clear, cooler, and sunny

(C) warmer and mostly cloudy

(D) snow

20. Fatima went to the library. She looked up the average amount of rain that fell in Macon, Georgia, during the month of November for each of the last ten years. What can she predict with this information?

(F) She can predict about how much it will rain in Macon, Georgia, next April.

(G) She can predict about how much it will rain in Chicago, Illinois, next November.

(H) She can predict about how much it will rain in Macon, Georgia, next November.

(J) She can predict about how much it will rain in Dalton, Georgia, next November.

21. An item that blocks the passage of light is _____ .

(A) translucent

(B) transparent

(C) opaque

(D) none of the above

22. A twist-off bottle cap is an example of what type of simple machine?

(F) a wheel and axle

(G) a screw

(H) a pulley

(J) a wedge

23. A set of stairs is an example of what type of simple machine?

(A) a pulley

(B) a screw

(C) an inclined plane

(D) a lever

24. What type of simple machine do you use when you raise and lower blinds?

(F) a pulley

(G) an inclined plane

(H) a wheel and axle

(J) a lever

25. A bottle opener is an example of what type of simple machine?

(A) a screw

(B) a lever

(C) an inclined plane

(D) a wedge

26. A palm tree is an example of a _____ .

(F) producer

(G) consumer

(H) decomposer

(J) community

27. A decomposer is an organism that _____ .

(A) lives by feeding on other organisms

(B) feeds on the remains of other organisms

(C) makes its own food

(D) none of the above

GO

28. In a predator-prey relationship, when the predator population decreases, the prey population will probably _____ .

(F) increase

(G) decrease

(H) stay the same

(J) not enough information to know

29. What is an adaptation?

(A) a trait or ability that helps an organism survive in its environment

(B) the number of pairs of genes a particular organism has

(C) the ways in which an organism can travel

(D) an organism's place in the food chain

30. An example of an adaptation would be _____ .

(F) a dog shedding its heavy coat in the summer

(G) the thorns on a rose bush

(H) a tiger's sharp teeth and claws

(J) all of the above

31. One example of an adaptation in catfish is that they have dark backs and light bellies. How might this help them survive?

(A) It helps them find food on the bottom of the lake.

(B) It helps turtles find them.

(C) It makes them less visible to prey from above and from below.

(D) It makes them taste better.

32. Some organisms have special adaptations that help them blend into the background of their environment so that predators can't see them. This is called _____ .

(F) blendability

(G) camouflage

(H) selection

(J) fusion

33. Which of the following is an example of camouflage?

(A) A skunk can spray an unpleasant scent to protect itself from predators.

(B) A young joey grows and develops in its mother's pouch.

(C) A stick insect resembles the twig on which it sits.

(D) An anteater has a long, slender snout and a long tongue, which it can thrust into anthills.

STOP

Name _____   Date _____

Final Science Test
Answer Sheet

1 Ⓐ Ⓑ Ⓒ Ⓓ
2 Ⓕ Ⓖ Ⓗ Ⓙ
3 Ⓐ Ⓑ Ⓒ Ⓓ
4 Ⓕ Ⓖ Ⓗ Ⓙ
5 Ⓐ Ⓑ Ⓒ Ⓓ
6 Ⓕ Ⓖ Ⓗ Ⓙ
7 Ⓐ Ⓑ Ⓒ Ⓓ
8 Ⓕ Ⓖ Ⓗ Ⓙ
9 Ⓐ Ⓑ Ⓒ Ⓓ
10 Ⓕ Ⓖ Ⓗ Ⓙ

11 Ⓐ Ⓑ Ⓒ Ⓓ
12 Ⓕ Ⓖ Ⓗ Ⓙ
13 Ⓐ Ⓑ Ⓒ Ⓓ
14 Ⓕ Ⓖ Ⓗ Ⓙ
15 Ⓐ Ⓑ Ⓒ Ⓓ
16 Ⓕ Ⓖ Ⓗ Ⓙ
17 Ⓐ Ⓑ Ⓒ Ⓓ
18 Ⓕ Ⓖ Ⓗ Ⓙ
19 Ⓐ Ⓑ Ⓒ Ⓓ
20 Ⓕ Ⓖ Ⓗ Ⓙ

21 Ⓐ Ⓑ Ⓒ Ⓓ
22 Ⓕ Ⓖ Ⓗ Ⓙ
23 Ⓐ Ⓑ Ⓒ Ⓓ
24 Ⓕ Ⓖ Ⓗ Ⓙ
25 Ⓐ Ⓑ Ⓒ Ⓓ
26 Ⓕ Ⓖ Ⓗ Ⓙ
27 Ⓐ Ⓑ Ⓒ Ⓓ
28 Ⓕ Ⓖ Ⓗ Ⓙ
29 Ⓐ Ⓑ Ⓒ Ⓓ
30 Ⓕ Ⓖ Ⓗ Ⓙ

31 Ⓐ Ⓑ Ⓒ Ⓓ
32 Ⓕ Ⓖ Ⓗ Ⓙ
33 Ⓐ Ⓑ Ⓒ Ⓓ

Answer Key

Page 8
1. D
2. G
3. A

Page 9
1. Ralph is a dog.
2. No. He is dirty and hungry.
3. Yes. He is wearing an old collar with an identification tag.
4. He was hungry.
5. She does not like Ralph. She sprays him with the hose and swats at him with a broom.

Page 10
1. evening
2. on a beach
3. Gabe, Hannah
4. Gabe can't identify a creature he found on the beach.
5. Gabe will probably ask to meet Hannah's older sister and learn more about horseshoe crabs.

Page 11
1. Samantha. Today is her birthday.
2. Samantha's mother. She refers to Samantha's "father and me."
3. Samantha's sibling (brother or sister unknown). The passage refers to Mom and Dad.
4. A

Pages 12–13
1. M, S, S, S
2. Sollie is athletic and graceful, but sinks in the water and was being thrown around behind the boat when he forgot to let go of the rope.
3. B
4. Answers will vary. One possible answer: like a dolphin racing down the coast.
5. Sollie is a seal, sleek and smooth in the water.
6. H

Page 14
1. B
2. G
3. A
4. H
5. B

Page 15
1. A
2. The theme is why the sun and moon appear in the sky.
3. J
4. The moral is that a person sometimes pretends that he does not want something that he or she cannot have.

Page 16
1. pillows
2. children
3. three
4. play, day
5. the second and fourth lines
6. 6, 6, 6, 5

Page 17
1. D
2. G
3. A
4. G

Page 18
Fahrenheit—invented by Gabriel Fahrenheit; water freezes at 32°F; normal body temperature is 98.6°F; water boils at 212°F.
Celsius—invented by Anders Celsius; water freezes at 0°C; normal body temperature is 37°C; water boils at 100°C.

Page 19
1. A
2. G
3. B
4. H
5. D

Page 20
1. B
2. J
3. T, F, T, F

Pages 21–22
Mini-Test 1
1. C
2. J
3. D
4. F
5. C
6. J
7. D
8. F
9. C
10. G

Page 25
1. B
2. H
3. B
4. G
5. C
6. F
7. D
8. H

Page 26
1. B
2. G
3. A
4. H
5. D
6. H

Page 27
Students' sentences will vary. Sample sentences are listed below.
1. pre; We saw a preview of this movie at the theater.
2. un; The class was unhappy when the field trip was cancelled.
3. be; We should never belittle someone because he or she is different than us.
4. co; My mom's coworkers had a birthday party for her.
5. dis; She had a great distrust of strangers.
6. re; We will replay the game when the rain stops.

Page 28
1. C
2. F
3. C
4. G
5. D
6. F
7. C
8. F
9. A
10. F

Page 29
1. plane
2. write
3. sea
4. new
5. hear
6. four
7. know
8. bee
9. which
10. to
11. two
12. too
13. too
14. to
15. their
16. They're
17. there
18. there, their
19. They're
20. their

Page 30
1. C
2. J
3. C
4. G
5. B
6. J
7. D

Page 31
1. B
2. G
3. D
4. H
5. D
6. H
7. B
8. F

Page 32
Mini–Test 2
1. B
2. G
3. B
4. J
5. C
6. F
7. B

Page 35
1. C
2. F
3. Answers will vary.

Page 36
1–4. Answers will vary.

Page 37
1–4. Answers will vary.

Page 38
1–4. Answers will vary.

Page 39
1–4. Answers will vary.

Page 40
1. D
2. H
3. D
4. G

Page 41
1. B
2. F
3. B
4. F
5. C
6. F
7. C
8. H

Page 42
1. A
2. G
3. D
4. J

Page 43
1. C
2. H
3. D
4. J
5. A
6. J
7. C
8. F
9. C
10. F

Page 44
1. C
2. H
3. C
4. J
5. B
6. F
7. C
8. H
9. B
10. G

Page 45
Mini–Test 3
1. C
2. H
3. C
4. G
5. A
6. G
7. B
8. G

Page 47
1. D
2. H
3. B
4. H
5. B
6. Sample answer: Canada
7. Sample answer: Adam
8. Sample answer: Lake Erie
9. state
10. nouns: Yolanda, sister, school; pronouns: her
11. nouns: Karen, volleyball, friends; pronouns: I, our
12. nouns: father, Uncle Ken, meeting; pronouns: My, their
13. nouns: Toby, dress
14. nouns: Randy, Father, seeds

Page 48
1. red, yellow, her
2. Those, their, spelling
3. This, our, new
4. Both, birthday
5. My, busy
6. playful, frisky
7. these
8. two, that
9. two, one, red
10. My, bright, blue
11. smallest
12. twelve, fourteen, Kit's
13. his, shady, elm
14. badly
15. gently
16. surely
17. happily
18. swiftly
19. early
20. brightly
21. loudly
22. carefully

Page 49
1. B
2. J
3. B
4. G
5. A
6. F
7. B
8. H

Page 50
1. Tyson began singing "The Star-Spangled Banner."
2. Joe read an article about Canadian geese in a magazine called *Migrating Birds.*
3. We sold school supplies to help raise money for the Red Cross.
4. "I'm really glad you are here," Abby said.
5. D
6. H
7. A
8. G

Page 51
1. A
2. H
3. B
4. F
5. C
6. H
7. D
8. G

Page 52
1. po/ta/to
2. pro/vide
3. cir/cus
4. cloth/ing
5. cou/ple

6. dec/o/rate
7. de/stroy
8. dou/ble
9. fin/ger
10. hap/pen
11. height
12. ledge

Page 53
1. DE
2. DE
3. IN
4. EX
5. IM
6. DE
7. IM
8. IN
9. EX
10. DE
11. IN
12. IM
13. DE
14. EX
15. IN

Page 54
1. S
2. F
3. S
4. F
5. F
6. S
7. S
8. S
9. F
10. S
11. B
12. J
13. and
14. but
15. or
16. but
17. and
18. but
19. or

Page 55
Mini–Test 4
1. B
2. H
3. B
4. F
5. A
6. G
7. D
8. H
9. B

Pages 59–64
Final English/
Language Arts Test
1. C
2. G
3. B
4. F
5. D
6. H
7. B
8. G
9. B
10. F
11. C
12. G
13. A
14. H
15. A
16. J
17. C
18. H
19. A
20. H
21. A
22. F
23. B
24. J
25. A
26. G
27. C
28. J
29. A
30. F
31. B
32. J
33. A
34. J
35. B
36. G
37. A
38. G
39. A
40. F
41. C
42. F
43. C
44. H
45. B
46. H
47. B
48. F

Page 69
1. D
2. J
3. A

4. F
5. 82.56
6. 327.61
7. 59.44
8. 96.87
9. 4,021.37

Page 70
1. B
2. J
3. D
4. G
5. B
6. J
7. D
8. G

Page 71
1. 20
2. 80
3. 30
4. 20
5. 30
6. 90
7. 50
8. 100
9. 60
10. 80
11. 70
12. 50
13. 900
14. 500
15. 400
16. 300
17. 700
18. 200
19. 500
20. 700
21. 900
22. 400
23. 200
24. 500
25. 2,000
26. 7,000
27. 5,000
28. 5,000
29. 3,000
30. 9,000
31. 9,000
32. 8,000
33. 4,000
34. 6,000
35. 3,000
36. 3,000

Page 72
1. B
2. H
3. C
4. H
5. B
6. F
7. C
8. G
9. D
10. H

Page 73
1. 536
2. 66
3. 518
4. 344
5. 416
6. 7,790
7. 3,392
8. 1,176
9. 4,272
10. 6,048
11. 2,106
12. 3,942
13. 1,884
14. 2,191
15. 3,784
16. 18,105
17. 8,768
18. 54,203
19. 5,472
20. 28,899

Page 74
1. B
2. H
3. D
4. H
5. A
6. H
7. A
8. H
9. A
10. G
11. D
12. H

Page 75
1. 62
2. 4 R3
3. 169
4. 65
5. 6 R3
6. 15
7. 3 R2
8. 5 R3

9. 29
10. 40
11. 8 R2
12. 114
13. 9 R1
14. 8 R3
15. 213

Page 76
1. A
2. H
3. C
4. H
5. A
6. H
7. B
8. H

Page 77
1. 9.4
2. 7.9
3. 10.9
4. 7.9
5. 6.9
6. 2.7
7. 1.1
8. 5.3
9. 2.5
10. 2.4
11. 0.48
12. 0.59
13. 0.68
14. 0.79
15. 0.37
16. 2.91
17. 13.1
18. 49
19. 178.4
20. 12.1
21. 15.3
22. 21.2
23. 18.2
24. 6.1
25. 340.2
26. 62.8
27. 186.9
28. 6.2
29. 1.6
30. 284.2
31. 62
32. 9.2

Page 78
1. 4
2. $\frac{2}{6}$
3. $\frac{3}{9}$

4. $\frac{6}{8}$
5. 4
6. 4
7. 3
8. 10
9. 8
10. 5

Page 79
1. B
2. H
3. C
4. H
5. A
6. H

Page 80
1. B
2. G
3. C
4. G
5. A
6. J
7. A
8. G
9. A
10. G

Page 81
1. C
2. A
3. C
4. A
5. C
6. C
7. 3×4
8. $5 + 6 + 8$ or $8 + 6 + 5$
9. $(7 \times 4) \times 3$
10. $(4 \times 3) \times 7$ or $(3 \times 4) \times 7$ or $7 \times (3 \times 4)$
11. $8 + (4 + 2)$
12. $2 + (8 + 4)$ or $2 + (4 + 8)$ or $(4 + 8) + 2$

Page 82
1. $(2 \times 6) + (2 \times 3)$
   $2 \times 9 = 12 + 6$
   $18 = 18$
2. $(3 \times 4) + (3 \times 3)$
   $21 = (4 + 3)3$
   $21 = 21$
3. $(4 \times 9) - (4 \times 1)$
   $4 \times 8 = 36 - 4$
   $32 = 32$

4. $(9 \times 2) - (3 \times 2)$
   $12 = (9 - 3)2$
   $12 = 12$
5. $(2 \times 15) - (2 \times 3)$
   $12 \times 2 = 30 - 6$
   $24 = 24$
6. $(7 \times 8) + (5 \times 8)$
   $12 \times 8 =$
   $56 + 40$
   $96 = 96$
7. $(5 \times 5) - (3 \times 5)$
   $10 = (5 - 3)5$
   $10 = 10$
8. $(3 \times 5) + (3 \times 6)$
   $3 \times 11 =$
   $15 + 18$
   $33 = 33$
9. $(2 \times 4) + (3 \times 4)$
   $20 = 8 + 12$
   $20 = 20$

Pages 83–84
Mini-Test 1
1. C
2. H
3. B
4. H
5. B
6. H
7. C
8. G
9. D
10. H
11. C
12. G
13. A
14. J
15. D
16. H
17. B
18. G
19. D
20. G
21. A
22. H

Page 86
1. 32
2. 10
3. 240
4. 8
5. 160
6. 2.5
7. 12,000
8. 320
9. 4
10. 32 ounces

11. 1.25 tons
12. no
13. yes

Page 87
1. 10,000
2. 10
3. 2
4. 0.5
5. 7
6. 2,000
7. 3,000
8. 4.5
9. 3
10. 6
11. 40
12. 5
13. 10 stones
14. 35 cookies
15. 6 grams
16. 1,300 grams

Page 88
1. 90°
2. 15°
3. 50°
4. 60°
5. 137°
6. 105°
7. 70°
8. 55°
9. 35°

Page 89
1. 90°
2. 180°
3. 360°
4. 270°
5. 180°
6. 90°
7. 180°
8. 270°
9. 270°
10. 180°
11. 90°
12. 90°
13. 360°
14. 90°
15. 180°
16. 270°
17. 90°
18. 90°
19. 270°
20. 360°

Page 90
Mini-Test 2
1. A
2. J
3. A
4. H
5. B
6. J
7. C

Page 92

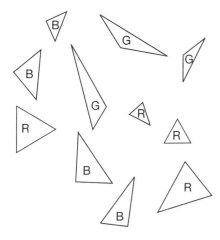

Page 93
1. B
2. H
3. D
4. H
5. B
6. G
7. A
8. J

Page 94
1. rhombus
2. rectangle
3. trapezoid
4. quadrilateral
5. square
6. parallelogram
7. quadrilateral
8. trapezoid

Page 95
1. D
2. G
3. B
4. D
5. G
6. B

Page 96
1. cylinder
2. sphere
3. cone
4. none of these
5. sphere
6. sphere
7. cylinder
8. cone
9. none of these
10. cone
11. none of these
12. sphere

Pages 97–98
1. boat
2. picnic basket
3. acorn
4. frog
5. butterfly
6. fish
7. worm
8. lily pad
9. flower
10. bird
11. leaf
12. rock
13–16. Check students' placement of items on graph.

17. Students' graphs should resemble evergreen trees.
18. C
19. Students' graphs should resemble the letter P.
20. F

Page 99
Mini-Test 3
1. A
2. F
3. B
4. H
5. A
6. H
7. C
8. G

Page 100
1. 21; Rule: Add the two previous numbers to get the next number.
2. 32; Rule: Add by increasing consecutive integers (each successive number is 1, 2, 3, etc.).
3. 62; Rule: Subtract by integers increasing by threes (3, 6, 9, etc.).
4. 17; Rule: Alternate adding and subtracting by increasing integers (1, 2, 3, 4, etc.).
5. 45; Rule: Add the number to itself and subtract 1.
6. 44; Rule: Add by integers increasing by fours (4, 8, 12, etc.).
7. 89; Rule: Subtract by increasing consecutive integers (1, 2, 3, etc.).

8. 71; Rule: Add by increasing even integers (2, 4, 6, etc.).
9. 51; Rule: Subtract 3, add 2, repeat.
10. 78; Rule: Add 5, subtract 8, repeat.

Page 102
1. B
2. H
3. D
4. H
5. A
6. H
7. A
8. J
9. B

Page 103
Mini-Test 4
1. C
2. 32, 64, 128, 256, 512; Rule: Multiply each new number times 2.
3. 56, 63, 70, 77, 84, 91, 98, 105
4. F
5. C
6. F
7. B
8. F
9. D

Page 105
1. C
2. F
3. A
4. F
5. D
6. H

Page 106
1.

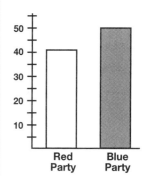

2.

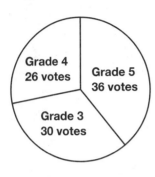

Grade 4
26 votes

Grade 5
36 votes

Grade 3
30 votes

3. The bar graph shows total votes for the red party and for the blue party; it does not break down the votes by grade. The circle graph shows the number of votes per grade; it does not show the party for which the votes were cast.

Page 107
Mini-Test 5
1. D
2. J
3. C
4. H
5. D
6. G

Pages 109–110
1. D
2. G
3. A
4. G
5. C
6. G
7. 175 − 161 = 14 or 2 × 7 = 14
8. D
9. H
10. C
11. H
12. B

Page 111
1. C
2. H
3. D
4. F

5. D
6. F
7. B
8. F

Page 112
1. D
2. H
3. B
4. G
5. A
6. 25 + 13 = 38
7. H
8. 47.82 − 25 = 22.82

Page 113
Students should describe how they solved each problem. Answers are:
1. 159 calories
2. $\frac{5}{8}$
3. 3 balloons
4. 23 cars
5. $15.00
6. $1.79

Page 114
1. D
2. G
3. C
4. H
5. C
6. G
7. D

Page 115
1. B
2. H
3. D
4. H
5. B

Page 116
Mini-Test 6
1. D
2. G
3. B
4. H
5. C
6. H
7. C

Pages 119–123
Final Mathematics Test
1. C
2. F
3. B
4. F
5. D
6. F
7. B
8. F
9. C
10. G
11. C
12. H
13. B
14. F
15. C
16. J
17. D
18. G
19. A
20. J
21. B
22. F
23. B
24. F
25. D
26. G
27. D
28. F
29. C
30. F
31. B
32. F
33. B
34. J
35. B
36. J
37. B
38. F
39. B
40. J
41. C
42. J
43. A
44. F
45. C

Page 128
1. C
2. F
3. B
4. J

Page 129
1. B
2. J
3. B
4. J
5. C
6. F
7. C
8. G
9. D

Page 130
1. B
2. H
3. B
4. F
5. D
6. G
7. A

Page 131
1. A
2. G
3. D
4. H

Page 132
1. B
2. H
3. D
4. F
5. C
6. G
7. A
8. J

Page 133
1. A
2. H
3. C
4. G
5. C
6. H

Page 134
1. The goal of the abolitionist movement was to end slavery.
2. B
3. The goal of the women's suffrage movement was to gain women the right to vote in the United States.
4. J

Page 135
Mini-Test 1
1. D
2. G
3. C
4. G
5. D
6. G
7. C
8. H
9. B

Page 137
1. b
2. c
3. f
4. a
5. d
6. e
7. i
8. g
9. h

Page 138
1. A
2. H
3. C
4. G
5. B
6. J

Page 139
Mini-Test 2
1. D
2. G
3. B
4. H
5. B
6. H
7. B
8. J

Page 141
Students' paragraphs will vary but should describe how the right to life, liberty, and the pursuit of happiness are applicable to people's lives today.

Page 142
1. Students' paragraphs will vary but should describe how freedom of expression is important in a democracy.
2. Students' paragraphs will vary but should describe ways that their lives would be different if one of these freedoms was taken away.

Page 143
1. A
2. G
3. D
4. G
5. C
6. G
7. B
8. H

Page 144
1. C
2. J
3. Answers will vary. One possible answer: Voters have a responsibility to understand the issues and know where the candidates stand on them before voting.
4. Answers will vary. Students should mention that William has the right of free speech, which Jane did not respect by trying to stop his actions. William respected others' views by not forcing his booklet onto them if they were not interested.

Page 145
Students' paragraphs will vary but should illustrate positive character traits of the person they chose to write about.

Page 146
Mini-Test 3
1. B
2. F
3. C
4. G
5. C
6. G
7. B
8. H

Page 148
1. C
2. G
3. D
4. F
5. Answers will vary, but students should indicate that if each family specialized, they would have more time to develop and improve their productivity of the one item.

Page 149
1. C
2. J
3. A
4. G
5. B
6. H
7. A
8. Answers will vary. Students may mention that some items are more costly than what they currently have available to them in their funds. Therefore, they must save for those items over time. They might also mention that they may encounter unexpected expenses, and a savings account will provide the funds necessary to pay these expenses.

Page 150
Mini-Test 4
1. C
2. H
3. B
4. G

Pages 153–156
Final Social Studies Test
1. C
2. F
3. D
4. F
5. B
6. G
7. A
8. H
9. B
10. G
11. D
12. H
13. A
14. F
15. C
16. G
17. B
18. H
19. A
20. J
21. B
22. H
23. B
24. J
25. B
26. H
27. D
28. F
29. B
30. J
31. C
32. G
33. A
34. H
35. C
36. J

Page 161
1. B
2. H
3. D
4. F
5. A

Page 162
1. B
2. H
3. A
4. J
5. A
6. J
7. B
8. H

Page 163
1. U
2. S
3. S
4. U
5. U
6. S
7. S
8. U
9. U
10. S

Page 164

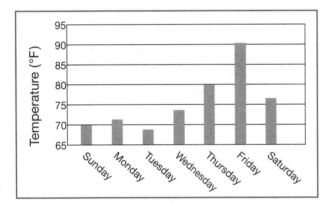

The pattern of change is irregular.

Page 165
Answers will vary. Students should list five sources, and these sources should reflect a variety of source material (e.g., they should not all be books). They should include a brief description of the type of information about glaciers that they found in each source.

Page 166
1. B
2. G
3. A
4. F

Page 167
Mini-Test 1
1. A
2. H
3. B
4. G
5. D
6. G

Page 169
Students should mention that Terry did his second experiment a month later, in September, which meant the plants received less sunlight than the ones in the first experiment. He forgot to take this factor into account when repeating his study.

Page 170
1. C
2. F
3. B
4. G
5. A
6. J
7. C
8. F

Page 171
Mini-Test 2
1. A
2. G
3. A
4. F
5. C
6. J
7. B
8. G
9. A

Page 173
1. B
2. C
3. E
4. A
5. D

Page 174
1. C
2. G
3. D
4. H

Page 175
1. Mercury
2. Venus
3. Earth
4. Mars
5. Jupiter
6. Saturn

7. Uranus
8. Neptune
9. Pluto

Page 176
1. A
2. H
3. B
4. H
5. B
6. J
7. A
8. F
9. A
10. J

Page 177
1. C
2. J
3. A
4. F
5. A
6. G
7. C

Page 178
Mini-Test 3
1. A
2. H
3. D
4. G
5. C
6. G
7. C
8. F

Page 180
1. B
2. F
3. C
4. G
5. A
6. G
7. D
8. G
9. D

Page 181
1. A
2. G
3. D
4. H
5. B
6. F
7. D
8. J

Page 182
1. C
2. G
3. C
4. F
5. D
6. G
7. A
8. F
9. B

Page 183
Mini-Test 4
1. B
2. H
3. D
4. J
5. C
6. F
7. C
8. G

Page 185
1. B
2. H
3. A
4. G
5. A
6. Answers will vary. Students may mention that most of the desert plants and animals, such as cacti and reptiles, might die because they are accustomed to warmer temperatures.
7. Answers will vary. Students may mention that certain animals and plants that are used to cooler temperatures might thrive. These organisms might have trouble finding food if their usual sources die off in the colder environment.

Page 186
1. b
2. f
3. e
4. l
5. g
6. a
7. d
8. j
9. h
10. i
11. k
12. c

Page 187
Mini-Test 5
1. producer
2. consumer
3. decomposer
4. consumer
5. consumer
6. producer
7. decomposer
8. producer
9. B
10. G
11. C
12. J
13. A

Pages 190–193
Final Science Test
1. A
2. H
3. C
4. H
5. A
6. G
7. C
8. G
9. D
10. F
11. A
12. G
13. C
14. F
15. D
16. J
17. C
18. G
19. B
20. H
21. C
22. G
23. C
24. F
25. B
26. F
27. B
28. F
29. A
30. J
31. C
32. G
33. C

NOTES

NOTES

NOTES

NOTES

NOTES